T0018988

Praise for *The Elements of Spellcrafting*:

"*The Elements of Spellcrafting* is a no-nonsense guide to practical sorcery, blending tradition and innovation without extraneous blather or hyperbole. With humour and much-needed down-to-earth advice, Jason Miller guides the reader through the key elements of effective magical practice."

—Phil Hine, author of *Condensed Chaos*, *Prime Chaos*, and *Pseudonomicon*

"In this practical, results-oriented manual, Jason Miller delivers more good advice per page than some entire books. The style is engaging, the writing clear and the lack of dogma refreshing. Highly recommended."

—Jake Stratton-Kent, author of the *Encyclopedia Goetica*

"This is one of those books of magic, far too rare, that make me want to stand up and applaud. Miller is not one for airy theorization. He's a practical magician and he keeps his sorcerous tires firmly on the pavement, as he lays out the common misconceptions and errors that magicians make, and best of all, the beneficial techniques that magicians often have to stumble onto themselves. Those new to magical practice will find this book a handy inoculation against nonsense and a guide through thickets of time-wasting foolishness. Those old hands at magic will find themselves thinking 'oh, so that's why that didn't work—of course!' It's a time saver and a breath of fresh air, clearing away the clouds of incense, all with humour, humility, and frank clarity. This is a book that makes you want to do magic."

—Patrick Dunn, author of *Magic, Power, Language, Symbol* and *The Practical Art of Divine Magic*

"Poignant and precise, well-articulated and presented with steady pace; Jason Miller once again delivers a magical manual for modern practitioners who want to go deeper and get more out of their witchcraft. Full of newly developed material, wit, and a confident tone, *The Elements of Spellcrafting* is a new take on advanced witchcraft and spellcraft that will expand your practice and point you in the direction of power and success. This is not a book I would lend out, you will never see it again!"

—Devin Hunter, author of *Witch's Book of Power* and *Witch's Book of Spirit*

"Sage, salt of the earth instruction for witches and occultists at all levels. Don't be afraid to ask for more than you deserve and now with this book, you'll have a plan rooted in witchcraft as well as practicality to achieve it!"

—Deborah Castellano, author of *Glamour Magic*

THE ELEMENTS
of
SPELLCRAFTING

THE ELEMENTS
of
SPELLCRAFTING

21 KEYS TO SUCCESSFUL SORCERY

JASON MILLER

This edition first published in 2017 by or New Page Books,
an imprint of Red Wheel/Weiser, LLC
With offices at:
65 Parker Street, Suite 7
Newburyport, MA 01950
www.redwheelweiser.com
www.newpagebooks.com

Copyright © 2017 by Jason Miller
All rights reserved. No part of this publication may be reproduced or transmitted
in any form or by any means, electronic or mechanical, including photocopying,
recording, or by any information storage and retrieval system, without permission in
writing from Red Wheel/Weiser, LLC. Reviewers may quote brief passages.

ISBN: 978-1-63265-120-4

Library of Congress Cataloging-in-Publication Data
Names: Miller, Jason, 1972- author.
Title: The elements of spellcrafting : 21 keys to successful sorcery / by
Jason Miller.
Description: Wayne, NJ : New Page Books, a division of The Career Press,
Inc., [2018] | Includes bibliographical references and index.
Identifiers: LCCN 2017048730 (print) | LCCN 2017050645 (ebook) | ISBN
9781632658869 (ebook) | ISBN 9781632651204 (pbk.)

Subjects: LCSH: Incantations. | Occultism. | Witchcraft. | Magic.
Classification: LCC BF1558 (ebook) | LCC BF1558 .M55 2018 (print) | DDC
133.4/4--dc23 LC record available at https://lccn.loc.gov/2017048730

Cover photograph © Matthew Brownlee
Background cover image by agsandrew/shutterstock
Interior photos/images by Matthew Brownlee
Interior by Lauren Manoy
Typeset in Adobe Garamond Pro and Koch Antiqua

Printed in Canada
MAR

10 9 8 7 6 5 4 3 2 1

Seneca once said, "While we teach, we learn."
This book is dedicated to the students of Strategic Sorcery.
Without you, this book would not have been possible.

Contents

Part 3: Advancing Your Craft

Acknowledgments

First and foremost, I wish to thank my wife and children for their patience and encouragement during the writing of this book. A very special thanks to my best friend and first student, Artist and Sorcerer Mathew Brownlee for providing the art for this book. It was a great time sitting at the bar, coming up with the comics for all the keys.

Thanks to all my initiators, mentors, teachers, friends, and informants who have revealed to me the secrets of their craft. Special thanks for this go to John Myrdhin Reynolds, Namkhai Norbu, Lopon Tenzin Namdak, Kunzang Dorje Rinpoche, Cliff and Misha Pollick, catherine yronwood, Tau Nemesius, Dr Jim, Paul Hume, and Blanch Krubner. You all opened yourselves up as mentors for me as a young man, and I would not be anywhere close to where I am today without your guidance.

Thanks to Joseph Peterson for allowing use of his images from his Noblet Tarot Reproduction.

Perhaps more than anyone, I need to thank the students of the Strategic Sorcery course, Sorcery of Hekate course, and all the other programs that I run. Your stories and field reports impacted this book a lot, and I continue to learn every day through teaching. I would not be able to lead the life I do without you, so thank you.

All of my books are guided by spirits, with one standing out as the patron of the book. This book owes much to St Cyprian of Antioch,

Sorcerer and Saint, Martyr and Mage, Bishop and Witch and Magus all. Please continue to bless my writings, and the work of those who read them.

Lastly, I want to thank all at New Page Press that worked on this book, specifically Laurie Kelly-Pye, who suggested I start writing books, and her husband, Michael, who was extremely generous with deadline extensions.

Introduction

Some Witches and Magicians think spells are something to be left behind, a phase that you pass through at the beginning of your path, eventually to be cast aside for more spiritual pursuits. Ideas of using Magic to find money or love, win against a rival, heal an ailment, secure the home, and turn the wheel of fate in your favor get abandoned as a youthful endeavor, or perhaps something that you stoop to as a last resort in an emergency. For these folks, Spellcrafting is certainly not something that you spend time on as an adult. Call me childish then, because I am not one of these folks.

I *love* Spellcrafting.

I have been practicing Magic and Witchcraft for nearly 30 years. I have dedicated the last of those three decades to teaching what I call Strategic Sorcery, and made a nice career of it too. I have seen remarkable results and flabbergasting failures. I have been party to rituals that saved lives, and others that blew them up. I have learned something from each spell about what works and what doesn't. I am not claiming to be the smartest, the most powerful, or the wisest Sorcerer on the block—in fact, I know that this is not the case. But I have seen some shit, dear reader, and have learned a lot from it.

I think most people who try spells know that they work. A little extra money comes in, a person they are attracted to shows interest back, a health condition improves. Spells work enough to convince the caster that Magic is real, but it is rare that the result is anything that would actually change one's life for the better in a significant way. This is what this book is about.

If people have ever asked you something like, "If spells work, why aren't you more successful?" this book is for you. The issue is not with the Magic itself, but with the application. If you apply these keys skillfully, no one will ever ask you again.

What follows is a list of 21 Keys that show both how to do effective Magic and to apply it in ways that matter—not just for solving a problem at hand, but for building a life filled with worldly success, spiritual fulfillment, and profound meaning.

Three Parts of This Book

The book is divided up into three parts:

In the first section, Setting Up the Spell, I layout the elements of planning that will help ensure success in your work. This involves having a firm grasp on what spells are capable of accomplishing, looking for the "enchantable points" that can be best affected by Magic, and some advice on how best to form spell strategy for maximum impact on those points.

The second section, Execution, details some of the key considerations involved in actually casting spells. Many of these involve regular practices that will impact any Magic you do, and others are about how to weave different spells together to approach the same goal from different angles. We will turn some of the old nuggets of common wisdom on their heads and show how there are other ways of thinking.

In the third section, Advancing Your Craft, I will lay out forward-thinking strategies that can optimize your craft for building a better life. This is the section that will take you from novice to master.

Oh, one other thing: There are comics that start every key to illustrate one of the points. There is no particular reason for this; I just like comics and think they're funny. Some people seem to think that books on

Magic should all be hardbound in basilisk leather with only very serious and arcane words. I, however, think Magic can be found in a nice, easily available book, with some snarky humor.

The Importance of Spellcraft

I don't suspect that many people know this, but an essay on Witchvox called "Spellcrafting, the REAL Witches' Craft" was the spark that ignited my career. I wrote it to refute two types of posts that were prevalent that month back in 2005. The first suggested that spells were detracting from the spirituality of Paganism and preventing it from taking its place among the world's great religions. The second were posts about how the details of Magic—the color of candles, the herbs, the words spoken—did not really matter and all that really mattered was *intention*.

To the first point, I simply must say that all religions have their Sorcery. In some, like Tibetan and Thai Buddhism, it is right out in front for all to see. In others, it is connected to a mystical strain of the religion, like Kabbalah within Judaism or Sufism within Islam. In yet others, it is folk-practice that, while not endorsed by the mainstream, still has a far reach. Examples such as various strains of Saint Magic throughout the Catholic world or Hoodoo within African American Protestantism also fit the bill. In short, Sorcery is everywhere.

In most cases, Magic and religion have an odd relationship where Magic attempts to control or mitigate the perils and pitfalls of life, while religion attempts to explain and give coping tools for when Magic fails. Magicians often fall afoul of religion for not conforming to dogma, and for usurping the power and connection to the world of spirit that is supposed to be the providence of the priest. Even within the mainstream religion, we may consider intercessory prayer as a type of Magic. Rituals are taken beyond simply praying, such as prayers repeated for a Magically important number of nights, or manipulation of statues and ikons, or the making of offerings are the first steps into spell work proper. The line between religion and Magic is blurry at best.

As to the second point that the Witchvox crowd was so fond of, that intention is the only necessary element in Magic, the idea is *hogwash* and kind of offensive. A Theban Magician did not painstakingly preserve and hide the Greek Magical Papyrii with its many formulas because intention was all that mattered. The Grimoires were not passed among a network of underground clergy and literate laity because the precise instruction did not matter. Families of African slaves did not preserve traditions of Congolese Magic in the New World at risk to their life just because your intention is all that matters! Yes, it's true that substitutions can be made and that Magic does not work through slavishly adhering to dogmatic instructions, but it's a bit disrespectful to suggest that the instructions do not matter.

What I Hope You Get Out of This Book

Magic works, and if you are reading this book, I assume you know or at least believe that already. If you don't know that already, I am not going to try to convince you. What I want you to get from this book is not just more instruction in how to perform Magic, but how to do it *well*.

Chances are that this is not your first book on Magic, Witchcraft, or the Occult, and you likely have enough spells on your shelf already. If you are a Magician, you have catalogues of dozens of spirits and instructions on how to conjure them. In this book, the focus will be on how to apply spells and how get the spirits to offer aid in meaningful ways. This information is what will make the difference between a life in which Magic provides some weird experiences and helpful coincidences verses a life in which Magic plays an integral role in realizing your true potential, achieving personal success, and giving back to the world.

—Jason Miller,
The Feast of St. Cyprian of Antioch, the Sorcerer Saint,
September 26, 2017

PART 1:
SETTING UP 1HE SPELL

7 KEYS FOR MAKING SURE THAT YOUR MAGIC WILL MEAN SOMETHING

Key 1:
Know What Magic
Actually Does

Before we can talk about the best ways to apply Sorcery to your life, we need to talk about what Magic can actually do. Because Magic is a subtle pursuit that is not even acknowledged as real by many people, this is not as clear as you might think, even to its practitioners.

By far, the most popular definition of Magic is from Aleister Crowley: "Magick is the Science and Art of causing Change to occur in conformity with Will."[1] Ever since Crowley set this definition down, people have been adding qualifiers to it to fit their particular spin. Dion Fortune seemed to be concerned that people would take some of the promises of traditional Magic too literally and lose track of the inner transformation she hoped Magic would cause, so she changed Crowley's definition to read "Magick is the art of causing changes **in consciousness** in conformity with the Will." Donald Michael Kraig, author of *Modern Magick*, was worried that Crowley was too broad and that his definition could be applied to literally anything, so he said, "Magic is the art and practice of causing change in accordance with will, **using methods not currently accepted by science.**"[2] Frater U.D. had an interest in pushing the Chaos Magic idea that altered states of mind are the key factor in working Magic so he added "Magic is the Science and Art of causing Change, on a material as well as a spiritual level, to occur in conformity with Will by **altered states of consciousness.**"[3] If you start Googling you can probably find a dozen or more spins on Crowley's definition, each reflecting a vested interest of the writer. Rather than add on to Crowley's classic definition, I would like to simply change a key word that I think instantly improves understanding of Magic and how to use it.

Magic Is an Influence, Not a Cause

If I could only change one thing about Crowley's definition it would be this: "Magick is the Science and Art of **influencing** change to occur in conformity with Will." The key here is to take out the idea that Magic is a direct cause of change, and instead make it an influence upon change— one influencing factor among many, the nudging of fortuna.

This is a much truer description of not just Magic, but almost any attempt at change. Whatever the effort, your influence is in competition with other influences, some of which support your goal, some of which work against it. If we are trying to sail a boat to Greece, we have the influence of the wind, the design of the sail, the quality of the boat, the skill of the other crew members, and a dozen other factors impacting the journey. When you extend this idea out, we can look at how the diet of the crew and events in their personal lives will impact the quest. We also have unforeseen events that may pop up that will have an impact: Something as large as a sudden storm or as small as a distracting glimmer have impact. Whatever action we take directly to make our sailing successful, it is set amidst this sea of influences.

When we get into Magical goals, the idea of **influencing** change rather than **causing** change is key. It shows us why spells that aim to divert a coming storm will work better than attempts to make it snow in July. One of these is an event that just needs a nudge, the other requires a drastic suspending of the laws of nature. Magic as an influence rather than a cause is why enchanting for a better job or to start a successful business is a good investment of time, while spells to win the Mega-Millions lottery are a fool's errand.

As far as modifying Crowley's definition of Magic further, I would even drop the "in conformity with will" line. That line speaks much more to Crowley's Thelemic philosophy than it does to the practical aspects of Magic. It also negates the not infrequent occurrences of accidental Magic manifesting in the lives of practitioners.

Influencing What Exactly?

So, if Magic is an influence rather than a cause, we need to think about *what* it influences. The answer isn't simple because sometimes truly miraculous things can happen, things that defy explanation. You do a spell for love and find someone sitting on your doorstep when you get home. You do some healing to reduce a tumor, and your next check-up has the doctors scratching their heads because they have never seen a reversal like that. One friend of mine, Sara Mastros,[4] conjured the spirit Sabnock, who according to the Goetia of Solomon, grants castles, and wound up moving into an apartment in the historic Henry Lister Townsend *castle* in Philadelphia. But scenarios like these are not the norm. These occasional and exceptional occurrences happen from time to time, but you can't bank on them. In general, Magic is an influence upon two things: **events** and **minds**.

By "events," I mean just about anything that has a probable chance of happening, from a storm, to a car accident, to a raise at work. Magic doesn't *make* these things happen, but it can influence them.

By "minds," I mean the classic enchantment of spellbinding—influencing what a person, or even groups of people, think. A lot of people get concerned that they might be robbing someone of free will by doing Magic for this, but it's important to remember that Magic is just an influence, like any other influence.

Because the mind seems subtle in comparison to hard-edged reality, and because some people believe Magic works primarily through a psychological mechanism, many assume that minds are easier to influence than external events. They are wrong.

If you have ever attempted to break a habit, you know how deeply intractable the mind can be, even from changes that you wish to make on yourself. The mind is even more resistant to influences from the outside. This is not to say that minds cannot be influenced with Magic. Enchantment is one of the oldest types of Magic, but it's rare that someone does a complete 180-degree turn on an issue just because of Magic. Enchanting people's minds is not difficult if it is for something that they are at least somewhat open to, and you do non-Magical things to help it along, but the idea that you are going to psychologically dominate someone through Magic and make them your psychic slave is not so easy to do, even if it were ethical. There are some over-the-top methods for this, but most people avoid them.

Sometimes you might be doing Magic that you expect to affect the mind of a target, but will instead manifest as an event. I first encountered this with a tanglefoot binding I did on a stalker. I thought the Magic would simply make them lose interest, but what happened is that during their stalking, they had an accident that put them in the hospital for a bit and provided enough evidence for a restraining order. The ladder that he was using to climb to her bedroom window collapsed, and he broke both his legs.

The Take-Away

Every key and every comic in this book presents a problem that people encounter when doing Magic. In this case, the problem is that we are told that Magic works, and that it always works, yet, obviously the world is not filled with Witches and Magicians who get everything they desire.

Magic always presents an influence on events and minds, but that influence is not always enough to sway the situation. Our Sorcerer, Harold, is trying to make it snow, probably so he can take off from work. Salphegor, the demon he has conjured, can influence the weather, but it's July, so snow is out of the question.

When crafting a spell, let your awareness of how Magic works inform what you use it for. When Magic doesn't work or work the way you think it should, ask yourself:

- ✪ What was I trying to influence, and how much resistance was there to it?
- ✪ Is there a more probable angle and manifestation that I can approach this from?
- ✪ Am I aiming to change minds, events, or both?

Key 2:
Stop Making Crappy Goals

Now that we have established that Magic is an influence on probable events and minds, we can start to plan our goals. When I started teaching, the first homework I gave was to set a long-term goal for something you wanted to change with Magic. After the first round of homework submissions, it became clear that I needed to give folks a little more guidance and specifically warn them about four types of crappy goals.

Impossible and Highly Improbable Goals

I hate to be the one to break this to you, but there are no spells that are going to make you physically invisible. Sorry, but you will have to put off your plans of Magical bank-robbing. That is what we call an impossible goal. Likewise, there is nothing I can do to change your physical appearance to look like Don Draper, create a girl for you like in *Weird Science*, manifest $100,000 overnight, turn you into a vampire that lives forever, or grant you telekinetic powers. You might be rolling your eyes or laughing at this, but I have been offered money to do all the above by people who believe that I can do them. Money that, of course, I did not take.

These are what we can aptly term *impossible goals*. It is not that miracles never happen or that paranormal phenomena do not ever manifest, but you shouldn't ever bank on them as a life plan. I don't care what the Grimoire says—it's probably not happening how you think it will. I think that most of you reading this probably understand this right at the outset, so I don't want to dwell on it.

Impossible goals are not the only problem though. Highly improbable goals are also crappy. Now, I am not talking about *hard* goals. I am talking about *very* highly improbable goals. The biggest and most common one is, of course, winning the lottery. When I assigned that goal-setting homework to students the first time, six out of 10 first submissions were some variation of wanting to win enough money in the lottery that they never have to think about money again.

The problem is that winning the lottery, while certainly possible, is highly improbable. At the time of this writing, Powerball estimates your chances of winning the jackpot at 1 in 292 million. Your chances of winning even just 1 million dollars are 1 in 12 million. To put this into perspective, you have a 1 in 9 million chance of being struck by lightning... twice. Your chances of being struck by lightning once this year are 1 in 960,000. This means, from the perspective of Magic influencing events, you are 300 times more likely to be successful with a spell to make someone get hit by lightning, than you would be at winning the Powerball jackpot.

While casting a spell to get someone struck by lightning *is* totally bad-ass, it's still highly improbable and not worth spending a ton of time on. So if winning the lottery is even less likely, maybe it's time to move on to something a little less difficult?

The Lame Goal

This is the opposite of the improbable goal. It is uninspiring and barely worth the effort. When students tell me that the thing they want to work on is becoming assistant manager of the paint store, pay down a $3,000 credit card bill, or, worse, tell me that they want to make more money *but not too much money*, it breaks my heart. Goals like this are fine as a stepping stone to somewhere else, and spells to get them done are absolutely in play, but as a goal that drives your Magic, it's kind of lame.

A good goal is inspiring. It lights a fire in the belly. It is a reason to charge into the temple at dawn, or head to the graveyard at 3 a.m. Just because we are not going for the impossible or highly improbable doesn't mean that we can't strive for greatness. Otherwise, what the hell are we doing?

We should not limit ourselves. Every now and then, someone tells me that they want to make more money, but *not* up in the six figures. Or that they want to make it as an actor or actress but *not* become a major celebrity. Why? Is there some benefit to others to *not* do these things? It is a matter of being afraid of success. That is never a good fuel for Magic.

Worse than that though, it cuts us off from our potential. What if the only way to make it at all is to make it *big*?

This is not true only of material success, either. It's also true for spiritual goals. We may think we are being humble by saying we only seek modest attainments, but examples of great people exist to *inspire greatness*, not just to be worshipped. In stories of the great Sorcerer turned Saint Milarepa, his attainment and wisdom seemed so far beyond his students that they insisted he must be the incarnation of some powerful Holy Man or Buddha. He scolded them and said that to insist that they were incapable of the same results that he achieved showed lack of faith in the teachings which promise enlightenment to any who dutifully practice.

Even if we do not become millionaires, or celebrities, or great Wisdom Saints, deliberately cutting ourselves off from that right at the start is no way to live your life. Yet all the time, people feel unworthy of great success and even uncomfortable at the thought.

Vague and Immeasurable Goals

The next type of crappy goal that we need to avoid is the vague and immeasurable goal. Things like "I want wealth," "I want to be healthy," and "I want to be enlightened." All are noble, but vague and immeasurable.

Let's take being rich as an example. If you evoke Tzadkiel, the Angel of Jupiter, and say, "My goal is to be rich," what is the metric that he is going to use? Maybe Tzadkiel looks at the world and sees that people who make over $40,000 a year are in the top 1 percent in the world, and then looks at you and your $60,000 a year and says, "You look pretty rich to me already." However, if you ask Tzadkiel to help you get promoted to a position where you are making $100,000 a year, as well as boost sales on your side web business by 30 percent this year, this is something specific that he can grab onto. It's also something you can measure yourself against.

Do you want to be "healthy"? Hey, me too! But what does that actually mean? If you are sick, do Magic to get rid of the sickness. If you are overweight, then you need to know how much you need to lose. What is going to be lost weight and what is going to be fat to muscle conversion? Should you do a spell for your long-term goal, or maybe a shorter-term goal for the first 20 pounds? However you do it, you should be able to measure it.

Enlightenment or "being more spiritual" is perhaps the hardest example to pin down, but even more important because if we don't at least try to determine what we mean, it just becomes meaningless fluff. Are we measuring our spiritual growth in terms of calm? In terms of insight? In terms of how well life goes for us as a sign of favor by the Gods? In terms of how many people we serve? In terms of our own happiness?

Whatever it is you are looking to do with your Sorcery, you should be able to measure it *somehow*. This is scary. It's putting your Sorcery where your mouth is. It is looking at the possibility of failing and having to admit that failure, but that's the only way we progress.

Setting Goals Is Not an Accomplishment

Did you set a good goal? That's awesome; I am happy for you. Do you feel like you accomplished something? Sorry, but you have not done *squat*! A few years back, I wrote a few posts about goal-setting on my blog and within the next couple a weeks received the following feedback:

> *"I worked really hard to set my Magical goal. I am going to hang this goal up in my temple. I feel like I have really accomplished something here."*

and

> *"Thank you for writing that. I feel like just reading it I have accomplished a lot!"*

or my personal favorite,

"Now that I have taken stock of my life and set some realistic goals for my success, I actually already feel successful. This is what I have been looking for! Thank you."

These quotes are presented in this book anonymously but with permission from the people who wrote them. All three people have one thing in common: After I checked back with them several months later, they all did exactly *nothing* to get closer to accomplishing their goals. This then is the last type of crappy goal: The one that is not acted on.

Goal-setting feels good and can feel like an accomplishment in and of itself. This is understandable; if you really take the time to examine your life, discover a lot of the self-sabotaging and negative inner scripts that you have been running, and take the time to figure out where you really want to be spiritually, materially, romantically, or socially, it can be a hugely satisfying and uplifting experience. It provides direction where formerly there was none.

It feels good.

It feels *really* good.

It feels as good as the day you first signed up for the gym membership and promised yourself that you would go three times a week. It feels good like the day you opened your Roth IRA. It feels good like the time you signed up for the dating seminar or the day you signed up for Weight Watchers.

The problem is you felt so good about just signing on to the idea that you decided to treat yourself to a little break. You did not end up going to the gym regularly. You did not end up contributing to the Roth IRA every year. You did not follow up the seminar by actually talking to anyone. You did not track your Weight Watchers points for more than a couple days.

Avoid fetishizing your goal. Your goal does not need to be written in a Moleskine bought specially for that purpose; it just needs to be accomplished. Sigilize the goal for a working, but don't obsess over it. Write it in whatever notebook you have on hand, and treat it with all the sacredness of your grocery list, because in the end it's just something that needs to get done.

So What's a Good Goal Then?

Hey, thanks for asking! Simply put, a good goal is pretty much anything you want to do with Magic that avoids these traps. You goal is difficult enough to warrant using Magic, but not so improbable that it would need a miracle. It's important enough to you that it inspires action. A great goal, in fact, seems to have its own gravity that pulls you toward it. Lastly, that goal is measurable. It's something you can look at and say, "Well, that worked!" or "That didn't work. Time to try something else."

In fact, there is a rule of thumb that will almost always keep your goals on track: **Make a plan that can happen without Magic. Then use Magic to make sure that it does**.

If you follow this one simple rule, you will never go astray. It will ground you into the world of difficult but achievable goals and keep your Magic aimed at things that you can measure—and thus adjust to as needed.

But I Don't Know What I Want!

Sometimes we really don't know what it is we want, making it hard to set these reasonable, inspiring, measurable goals I am writing about. That's okay. What you are looking for is commonly called Road Opening—a spell, ritual, or spirit to open new roads and opportunities in your life.

Road Opening is powerful because there is an asymmetric upside to more opportunities. Gordon White's excellent book *Chaos Protocols* goes deep into this and even goes so far as to say that Road Opening might be the only spell anyone really needs. Such is the power of opportunity.

I prefer to think of Road Opening Magic as the first step in Wayfinding. Wayfinding and navigation are different. Most of this book implies navigation: Finding your way from the point where you are now to the point where you want to be. In Wayfinding, one does not necessarily know the destination, just the type of place where you want to be or the direction you want to head in.

In Magic, Wayfinding starts with Road Opening, but soon invokes discernment through spiritual guidance, divination, and meditation as to which roads to travel. Road Opening without some Wayfinding will simply keep opening new opportunities, which is fine, but may prevent you from the harder commitments of keeping to a road that has now been opened where you can set your destination.

The Take-Away

The problem of this key is avoiding crappy goals. In the comic, Harold demanded wealth with no other specifics, a vague and immeasurable goal. Unless he had some avenue that wealth could manifest through, the millions he had in mind were probably also highly improbable. So, he found 10 bucks in some old clothes.

There are three things that I recommend you do after setting your goal:

1. Take action immediately after setting your goal. What is the first step?

2. Plan out the next several steps that you need to take after that first one, and assign them dates and times. If it doesn't have a date and time, it is not a real step.

3. A week later, look at your steps. If you did not do them when you said you would, you need to examine why. It usually either a) you realize that you don't want this right now as much as you say you do, or b) you need to figure out some way to keep yourself to it using pleasure/pain principals, because willpower alone isn't cutting the mustard.

Key 3:
Make Sure Your Life
Is Enchantable

Twelve years ago, I did a spell to get an extra $3,000 quickly. Shortly thereafter, I was in a traffic accident that was not my fault and the insurance payout for the damage was almost exactly $3,000. The car was still drivable, so I kept the three grand and used it for the vacation I wanted to take, but now I was stuck with a visibly damaged car.

Last year, I did a spell for an extra $10,000. I used a similar ritual. That month a high-profile client needed some extra work and consultations that resulted to just under $4,000, and I had an unexpected burst of people signing up for one of my courses that made up another $5,000. The last $1,000 came in through better-than-average book royalties. Why did this larger number come so easy when the lower number caused me an accident? Do the spirits like me better now? Am I just that much better at Magic? Maybe, but that's not it. The answer is that my life is currently more fiscally enchantable now than it was 10 years ago.

How Flexible Are You?

I cannot even begin to tell you how many people have Magical mishaps, failed spells, or just inconvenient results, like my accident, and immediately think that the Gods and spirits are mad at them. No one is mad at you. The spirits aren't playing games. Your Magic is not backfiring. Your life is just not set up to manifest the results that you asked for in a convenient way.

We know from the first key that Magic is an influence upon reality, not a reality-breaking force (usually). If you do a spell to get money, it is going to manifest through mundane means that have a logical explanation. The spell will have influenced those events, but it is not going to make it rain 20-dollar bills from the sky. If you plan on Magic having a role in your life, you need to be able to maximize the potential for that Magic to manifest in ways that you will appreciate.

So Ask Yourself: Is Your Life Enchantable?

Love Shows Up on the Doorstep

In 1946, noted rocket scientist Jack Parsons and one of his students, L. Ron Hubbard,[1] performed a series of Enochian workings in the desert, designed to bring Parsons a lover that he could practice sex Magic with. He specifically was looking for an "elemental women" with fiery characteristics. He came home from the desert and on his doorstep sat the 24-year-old red-headed beauty Marjorie Cameron.[2] They were instantly attracted to each other and allegedly spent the next two weeks in Jack's bedroom.[3]

This is an awesome story, of course, but most of the time our efforts at love Magic will not be immediately followed by lovers waiting for us on the doorstep, ready and willing to delve into some sex Magic. This seems like the exceptional result that happens with Magic every now and then. But was it that exceptional? Parsons' life was extremely enchantable in this regard. He owned and lived in a boarding house that catered to bohemian residents. It was one of his lodgers who brought Cameron over to the house. If Parsons was just a rocket scientist who spent most of his time in the lab, his efforts at finding his "elemental woman" might have taken longer, had a less spectacular result, or even completely failed. His life, however, was highly enchantable to this result.

When performing love Magic, there are a lot of ways to make your life more enchantable. The obvious one is to turn off the PlayStation, log off Facebook, and get out places that you might meet people. Unless, like Parsons, you run a boarding house, you will need to go out into the world to meet people. Join a club or organization so you can run into folks of similar interests. Volunteer, so you rub elbows with those who are also into giving their time to worthy causes. Talk to your neighbors or get involved in community activism so that the people you eventually want to spend more time with are a short drive away, rather than a plane ride away. And yes, if you must, join a dating site—no matter who you are, there is probably one that fits you. If there is a FarmersOnly.com, a ZombiePassions.com, and even a SeaCaptainDate.com, I am sure that there is someone out there for you. But when talking love Magic, it's not just getting out of the house that makes your life enchantable. It's you.

How do you look? How do you dress? Are you skilled at starting conversations? I am not telling you to become someone else; these are all skills that can be learned. I am also not telling you to become a pick-up artist or anything like that. Just make your life more enchantable by brushing up on social skills and grooming. You do not want your efforts at Sorcery to be thwarted by your lack of effort in the shower.

In fact let's make that our second rule of thumb: **Keep your Magical and mundane efforts pointed in the same direction.**

Financial Flexibility

So to get back to my story about the comparative money spells, why did my three grand have to be taken out of my car, when 10 years later I was able to conjure more than three times that amount with no ill effects?

When I did the first spell, I worked for a telecom in a position that did not offer bonuses or any sort of random income. If the company did well one month, I made the same amount of money that I did during months that the company did poorly. Money spells I did for small amounts always found a way to come through things like paid focus groups, short-term side jobs, unexpected gifts, bank errors, found wallets, and so on. In other words, penny-ante bullshit. Spells for larger sums or significant financial changes led to uncomfortably sudden job changes or things like the insurance payment for a car that I never got properly fixed.

Thankfully, I never experienced the "inheritance result" that so many people worry about as an outcome of money Magic. In fact, I have only ever encountered one person who this might have happened to, and the person who left the inheritance was already in hospice.

When I did the second spell last year, I worked for myself and drew my salary from the work I did. The path of least resistance for financial Magic is simply to have more customers, higher-paying purchases, or inspiration for a new product. In fact, one of my prior books was an idea that was the result of a money spell.

There are lots of ways to have flexible income other than running your own company. Some positions offer a combination of salary and commission. Some executives receive bonuses. Investments that pay dividends or day trading can be a great way to add an enchantable dynamic to your portfolio. Many people nowadays have small side businesses in addition to their daytime gigs. The combination of a regular paycheck from a day job with the variable or even passive income from assets and side gigs can be a wonderful way to get the money mojo moving.

Health Enchantability

Even in health matters, we have to make sure that our lives are enchantable. I had someone come to me asking for help with their acid reflux. I did some healing work related to White Tara and made him a talisman to keep under his bed, which is where he would have the attacks. Apart from the Magic, I told him to try to lose some weight, cut back on caffeine, try not to eat too late, and avoid trigger foods and drinks within six hours of bedtime. Most of all, he should see a doctor. A couple weeks later, he wrote back to thank me because his attacks diminished. A couple months later, though, the attacks were back. Sure enough, he was still using the talisman, but he started drinking late afternoon coffee, having after-dinner drinks, and generally not paying attention to any of the other stuff he needed to do. In fact, he started doing all these unhelpful things because he felt like the talisman would let him.

You might be thinking, "If I have to do all this other stuff to prevent attacks like this, why do I even need the Magic?" I know that's what the client was asking, albeit with more expletives. The answer is that Magic is an influence. It will help make the attacks happen less. It will diminish the severity of the attacks that happen. It will help you make the changes needed to stop them. It will not, however, permanently solve a problem that you keep perpetuating in non-Magical ways.

How enchantable is your body? How enchantable are your habits? How enchantable is your environment? These are the questions we need to ask when we do healing Magic. Magic, energy healing, and alternative medicine all help, but they are not going to re-write your DNA, replace your gut bacteria, or remove the need for effort and change on your part.

Dangers of Forcing Magic into an Unenchantable Situation

A few years back, a friend of mine hired a contractor to re-do her bathroom. She called on St. Expedite to get it done in a very short amount of time—like in a day or two. The problem is, despite what HGTV makes you think, under no circumstances would this have been possible. On day two of the remodel, a tub full of water wound up not in the tub, but in the living room, one floor down. Nutty stuff happens when you force Magic into impossible situations. This isn't "backfiring" so much as it is shooting a bullet into a room where the walls are all bulletproof and it ricochets 100 times.

A lot gets said about the dangers of Magic. Offended spirits, malefic curses, demonic obsession, and all the bogymen that people warn of can and do happen, but these are not the dangers of Magic that I am most concerned about. Way more problems come from Magic applied in un-skilled and counterproductive ways. That, to me, is a much larger danger than Asmodeus being pissed off at the type of incense you used. Try not to force a truly unenchantable situation with Magic.

When planning Magic, you should think of how your spell could possibly manifest. You don't have to steer it in that direction necessarily, as that would take away from avenues for manifestation that you may not be aware of at the moment. You do, however, have to think about how enchantable your life is toward any goal. If your life is not particularly open to the kind of Magic that you are doing, you need to realize that it may not manifest or perhaps just give underwhelming results. If you force the issue with stronger Magic and insistence, then be ready for life to blow up on you.

The Take-Away

In the comic on page 35, Harold wants to be attractive to the opposite sex, but apparently his life is not very enchantable in this regard, so Sal suggests washing up a bit as a start. The problem this key seeks to solve is forcing Magic to manifest in lives that are not easily adapted to enchantment. The solution is not always an easy one. It may require you to open a business, do some serious personal identity work, or even move to a new city where there are more opportunities than your current location.

My challenge for you is this: Instead of looking at your life through the lens of the Sorcerer who wants something, pretend that you are a demon that has been summoned. What would you have to do to make that happen for the Sorcerer that summoned you? What kinds of things would make your job more effective? Do those things.

Key 4:
Everything Matters

As I mentioned in the introduction, I was offered the deal for my first book, *Protection and Reversal Magick*, because of an article I wrote on Witchvox. All month, I was reading nuggets of wisdom like "colors of the candles don't matter—only your *intention*," "the exact herbs don't matter, only the *belief you put into it*," and "spirits and directions are just a *focus*, you don't actually need any of that stuff." Some folks even went so far as to suggest that spells didn't really work at all and are just psychological tools. In short, if you were new to the world of Magic and were reading Witchvox that month, you would walk away thinking that there is nothing at all necessary for Magic other than wishes and positive thinking.

Needless to say, that kind of thinking is crap. People all over the world did not painstakingly record formulas, spirit catalogues, and ritual procedures because "intention is all you need." Which brings me to the fourth key of successful Spellcraft:

Everything matters.

Yes, you read that right. Everything matters. Every damn thing.

The color of the candle? It matters.

The herbs you put in the bag? They matter.

The pronunciation of the names? They matter.

The incense you use...

The circle on the ground...

The wood for the wand...

The day...

The hour...

The direction...

EVERYTHING MATTERS.

Everything matters because that's not only how Magic works, it's how life works. If you had a calming tea this morning instead of coffee it affects how you interact with people—it matters. If I phrase this key one way verses another, it will affect your understanding of the points I make—it matters. There is no part of Magic or life that you get to ignore or replace without consequence.

Hexed by a Hexagram!

Years ago, a friend started a program of solar invocations every morning. Strangely, the more he did them, the more he felt heavy and depressed and sluggish. Eventually it started to affect his job and relationships in the exact opposite way than he had hoped. He asked me what I thought was happening, so I asked to observe his ritual. I noted that he was using a system of drawing Invoking or Banishing Hexagrams in the air where you invoke a specific planet based on the corner that you start from and the direction you go. The problem was that instead of drawing a *solar* Invoking Hexagram, he was drawing a *Saturn* Invoking Hexagram.

His *intent* was to invoke the sun. His spoken invocation was to the sun. His ritual actions, however, were invoking Saturn. If it was all in the mind, that shouldn't matter. If it was all about intent, that shouldn't matter. If it was a matter of pure will, that shouldn't matter. But it did matter.

Indeed, because the invocation was not to Saturn, and thus unable to direct the power toward a useful purpose, that Lead-like Saturnine vibe was dragging him way down. He changed the way that he was tracing his Hexagram in the air and soon things got a lot sunnier.

Stuff that Someone Else Just Made Up Probably Still Matters

In the previous example, we are faced with a conundrum. On the one hand, we have a case showing that what we hold in our own brain is not the only thing that matters in Magic—if it did, his belief that he was doing the correct hexagram and his intent for the ritual would have carried him through. On the other hand, are we willing to accept a universe in which hexagrams drawn from a certain point automatically invoke that planet, no matter what? Of course not.

The resolution of this seeming paradox comes when you understand that what mattered in this case was not his intent or some universal law, but the rules of tradition and ritual that he was operating within. There is no universal constant like gravity that makes the planets correspond to a certain point on the hexagram, or the elements to a point on the pentagram, or the herbs to a specific effect. Colors of the elements vary from tradition to tradition: Yellow indicates Air for Magicians rooted in the Golden Dawn style of practice, but indicates Earth to Tibetan Buddhists.

What mattered for my friend in the Saturn/solar debacle was that he decided to engage in a ritual style with certain protocols and rules within it. Even though these are not universal or inherently true, they still matter beyond just what he thought or intended. It was true in the current that he was standing in, and therefore true for him whether he willed it or not. This is one reason that some people report that the more they get involved in something like astrology, the more it effects them. They are standing in that tradition, in that current, and are therefore are playing by those rules.

Stuff that You Were Not Even Aware of Still Matters

Sometimes things you are not even aware of matter. I was given a text for a Naga Sang, a type of incense-offering ritual for serpent spirits of fresh water, from one of my teachers. These beings are very powerful and Magically useful, but they can be difficult to work with. They are fierce vegetarians to the point that even musk in their incense will drive them into a fury.

I started doing the offering ritual on the days that it was allowed, and followed all the typical taboos for the Nagas, but I started to experience some problems rather than signs of success. Money started to slow down. Plumbing problems manifested. The Nagas did not seem happy.

I talked to a fellow Tantrika about it, and they asked if I had eaten eggs in the last 24 hours. I eat eggs almost every morning. Because this offering rite forces a very close interaction with the Nagas than most, it was suggested that perhaps I should obey a further level of cleanliness and not eat any eggs. Also, I should cover my mouth with a Kata (an offering scarf) so that I am not blowing on the offerings when I make them. I made one offering following these rules, and the symptoms ended. Then I dropped this rite and went back to an offering with looser restrictions. Sometimes the hassle is not worth it.

The point is: Even though I was not aware of this level of taboo, it mattered.

Materia Matters

Recently I was doing some financial work for a client who owns a risk management firm. I had created a special oil lamp that contained High John for mastery, gravel root for constant work, licorice root for sweetening and influencing, bay for drawing money, and a host of other herbs, all placed within a bowl inscribed with Jupiter glyphs from financial Sorcery. The bowl is filled with oil and burned all day on the day of Jupiter every week.

Things worked well for a long period of time, and I would whisper the specific needs of my client to the spirit of the lamp. One month, my client informed me that they were going to be expanding and were worried about unnecessary expenses as their business worked through these growing pains. I whispered the request to the lamp, but the report from my client that month was unsatisfactory. Expenses were piling up fast.

I went back to the bowl and did some divination. I determined that although there was plenty of materia in the lamp to aid efforts of bringing in money, attracting new business, and keeping people happy, there was nothing in the mix that supported the goals of constricting costs. Because sassafras leaves are shaped like hands, they have often been linked with the ability to hold on to money. I even carry one in my wallet for this very reason. I went for a hike, gathered some leaves, and added them to the bowl. This time, my request was met with more success. I also added a small Saturn petition to restrict costs. Sometimes the spirits need a hand, and materia really does matter.

Slave to the Rules?

So, if everything matters, does that mean we have to follow every instruction in every tradition and every Grimoire? Even the ones that contradict each other?

No, of course not. That's what the next key is all about.

What I want you to remember for now is that very little in Magic is put there just to be "a focus." If the spell for St. Cyprian calls for Holy Water from seven churches, there is a reason that you should go to seven different churches and collect holy water from them. If the Grimoire asks for a wand cut at sunrise on a Wednesday morning, and this seems like old-fashioned claptrap that you don't really need, you should at least know the reason for it. (Hint: It's a wand associated with Mercury for communication with spirits.)

So the next time that you are at the Occult shop deciding whether you really need the green devil candle for the spell to collect debts, maybe go ahead and spring for it rather than just deciding that the white taper candle you already have is good enough, because you think *intent is all that matters.*

The Take-Away

In our comic, Harold used the wrong salt when summoning Salphegor, and now it looks like Sal is going to eat him. The problem that we are solving here is sloppiness. I have been involved in Magic and Witchcraft for nearly 30 years now, and there is a lot of sloppiness. I have been guilty of sloppiness myself, but nothing good ever came from it.

The solution is to realize that everything matters. Every single thing you omit affects the result. Everything you replace affects the result. Does that mean we have to slavishly follow some rules? No! I did not become a Sorcerer to slavishly follow rules to the letter. Maybe our omissions or replacements will just change it slightly, making the work sweeter instead of aggressive (look at the next comic). Maybe our changes will even make it better. But we don't really know until we know what the thing we are tweaking originally did and have a good reason for making our change. The one thing we know is that everything matters.

Key 5:
"Matters" Does Not
Mean Necessary

In the last key, we made the case that everything matters. I stand by that, everything *does* matter, but that doesn't mean that everything is *necessary*. The spell with the green devil candle will be *different* than the same spell performed without it. That doesn't mean you cannot do a debt collection spell without that green devil candle though; it will just be different. A green skull candle may get into the target's head a bit more. A green taper with the targets name written on it may get them to act more upright, or maybe it will, in fact, pack less of a punch.

Unfortunately, people are unable to grasp this nuanced teaching very easily. It is much easier to run to the extremes, and so most people fall into one of two camps: the ultra-traditional and orthodox, or the wildly (and often stupidly) eclectic.

For the ultra-traditionalists, the fact that someone wrote it is reason that it not only matters (which I agree with) but that It Is absolutely necessary and immutable (which I don't agree with). The older a text or tradition is, the more immutable and rigidly those instructions are taken. Any concession to time and place in which you are doing this Magic will, in their minds, sully the operation. Any concession to convenience is laziness. Any concession to innovation is betrayal and flakiness. Such is the orthodox view.

If a tradition or text has been delivered by a spirit or God in the past, then it is absolute. If the spirit or God delivers a revelation to a mystic or Sorcerer in the present, then it's assumed to be delusion, especially if it calls for changes or modernization of ancient methods. Gods forbid we actually act like it is the century that we are living in.

On the other side of the coin, we have the wild eclectics. For the wild eclectics, there is no higher authority than their own Gnosis. What passes for Gnosis can be anything from a mystical vision to a brain-fart. We will be talking about sane eclecticism later on, so I don't want to spend a lot of time on it now, but suffice to say that there is no part of a ritual or tradition that these folks think they cannot change or do without.

Between these two extremes runs a middle road, one where we recognize that people did not establish traditions for no reason and that everything matters, but where we also recognize that changing, replacing, modernizing, and streamlining things all have their place. Before we change things though, first we need to know what we are talking about.

Experience Before Change

What are you changing or getting rid of? The color of a candle? An oil? An herb that is hard to get or is poisonous? I completely understand; I work with Hekate a lot, but you won't find me messing around with aconite too much because it's toxic to the touch.

Maybe it's a whole section of a ceremony like purification or fasting that you have decided is antiquated or rooted in Christian thinking. Or perhaps it's forceful binding of spirits that you find too imperialistic. Maybe it's an offering that you object to or something that just seems like too much damn trouble. Whatever it is, you should make a decent attempt to understand what it is and what it does before you change it. That sounds obvious as I write it, but I cannot tell you how many times people have ditched or changed something without really understanding what they were changing. I can't tell you how many times I have done that myself, but that doesn't make it smart.

Ideally, you should have the firsthand experience of doing something at least a few times the traditional or written way before substituting or omitting. If you haven't done it, you don't fully understand it. You may think you do, but experience may prove otherwise. In 1996, I completed the months-long ritual to gain Knowledge and Conversation of the Holy Guardian Angel. Traditionally, this is followed by summoning the four Demon Princes and binding them—something that, at the time, I did not put any stock into or think necessary. My head was full of Aleister Crowley's Thelemic spin on Magic, and I thought the Holy Guardian Angel might be more like my "true will" than an actual being who would show up in the temple. This would make the demons similarly metaphorical, an allegory for our lower nature or base passions.

Eventually, the angel showed up and the first thing it told me was to get to work summoning those demons. What I did not understand, but which the angel made clear, is that I was inserting myself into a chain of manifestation, and that without binding those demons, wrathful spirits would be attracted to the angel and cause problems. You live and you learn. In this case, the lesson was whatever your operating theory of Magic is, it might be wrong. So if your theory tells you to dismiss something as superstition, or too pious, or unnecessary, that might also be wrong.

Of course, we cannot always take Magic and ritual for a spin. Sometimes the instructions call for something that is dangerous. Lots of people, including the famous traditional Witch Robert Cochrane, have died from wortcunning gone wrong. More than a couple Chinese emperors died of mercury poisoning from their alchemical longevity potions too. Other instructions may call for acts that we are morally opposed to. Animal sacrifice of chickens and farm animals is not really a big deal if you are used to killing animals for food anyway, but I hope no one reading this would justify drowning a cat as it instructs in a papyri spell that calls upon Hekate and Hermes.

Sometimes we may simply be unwilling or unable to follow tradition. So be it. You may be exactly right about not needing something or being able to replace it with something else. You may be wrong and willing to live with that, too. I'm not here to be the instruction police. I just want you to know what something does before you ditch it or change it.

Tweaking Your Thaumaturgy

Once you do your due diligence and know, or at least have a decent idea of, what something does and why it's there, you are free to tweak and make changes. But you don't make changes expecting it to be the same. You make your change because you know it will be different.

Let's say we are making an oil for influencing someone's mind and the ingredients call for calamus; if you replace it with licorice root you are still within the realm of influencing plants, but now it has a sweeter less aggressive touch. Or maybe you know that a spell calls for eggs to be offered to Hekate and you are a vegan, so you decide to offer dandelions instead—the spell may bring out a different aspect of Hekate based on the offering, one that is more necromantic because dandelions are associated with necromancy in some Greek sources.

There will also be times that you need to streamline things because they are just too long or needlessly complex. There is a business principal called Parkinson's Law that states tasks tend to expand the time available for their completion. When dealing with rituals designed for monks or full-time ritualists, it often becomes apparent that there are elements that are not necessary but have expanded to fill the time available. This happened with Tantra in Buddhism. Originally practiced by householders or wandering yogis, it was more Magic and yoga, but when it became mixed with the monastic traditions, the practices became more ecclesiastic and ornate. The problem is that when homeowners and yogis want to do it, they get taught to do the practices that the monks do, rather than those tighter practices from ages past.

There is nothing wrong with streamlining; often it can make a ritual better and more potent, as long as you know what you are doing and why. Disregarding or replacing elements of a ritual or spell because they require too much effort or because you don't think they matter is the mark of a dilettante. Knowing how to substitute or streamline to customize and optimize is the mark of a master.

The Take-Away

Whereas the problem the last key tried to address was sloppiness, this key addresses the problem of slavish repetition of the past and blind obedience. Taken together with the advice from the last key, we begin to see a middle road, one where we can clearly assess things from a position of knowledge and wisdom.

Harold still can't get his hands on volcanic salt, so he used sugar. This sweetened things up a bit, so Sal is not going to eat him anymore. What he is going to do instead I will leave up to your imagination. The point, though, is that you can substitute and get a result. It's just not going to be the same result. Everything matters, but not everything is necessary.

Key 6:
Make Skillful Statements
of Intent

If simple religion is asking for the will of God and the spirits to be done, then a part of what differentiates Magic is surely in asking for something specific to occur. This key is *crucial* to your success in Sorcery. The statement of intent drives the entire spell. It defines the parameters within which it operates, as well as the metrics for its success. This is a huge part of what makes Magic, yet even those with decades of experience under their robes give surprisingly little attention to what they are asking for. Whether you are standing in front of a demon, chanting over blessed and dressed candles in the dead of night, or raising and directing energy and mind, you should frame your intent as clearly and as carefully as if you were in front of some cartoon genii. You never want your last words to be "Genii, make me a ham sandwich!"

The Statement of Intent

Simply put, statement of intent is what you want a spell, ceremony, operation, or Magical strategy to do. If you have ever said a prayer asking for a Saint to heal you or tried to make a bargain with God for a pregnancy test not to be positive, you have made a statement of intent. But Magic is not just intercessory prayer or distressed bargaining, and just like in asking things of people, there are ways to ask that are skillful and there are ways to ask that are not.

Not long ago, a student of mine went through a lot of trouble to do an evocation of the spirit Bune from the Goetia of Solomon. This was an undertaking that was done as close to the book as possible and included a lot of time and effort. He asked for "increased income." That's it. Three hours of ceremony, a fair amount of expense, and more prep and study time than he could calculate to execute a beautiful and traditional rite, and that was the big request. The result is that within a week he got a raise of about a dollar an hour. Bune did its job—it fulfilled the request—it just didn't do it in a way that made a significant difference in his life.

It's easy to pick on others, but I have done this myself. All my early financial Magic was about "money drawing," and draw money it did:

the odd $20 found in the street, the opportunity to participate in focus groups that paid $50, a random gift from an aunt, or freebie furniture. I was excited that I did Magic and something happened, but when it came down to it, it was nothing that actually changing my life and sometimes wasn't even worth the effort.

Let's take a good look at noob, amateur, adept, and master statements of intent for someone looking for money.

Noob: Bring me money in a hurry!

Amature: Bring a new job!

Adept: Bring a career that offers steady and secure employment at no less than $X per year with the possibility of advancement.

Master: Bring opportunity for steady income that leaves $X per month after all bills, expenses, emergencies, and investments are made.

The noob statement leaves open the possibility of literally anything that gives just a little more than you had before. With the amateur statement, you leave open the possibility that you get a job that lasts for a couple hours one day clearing out some lady's yard. Probably not what you were hoping for, but technically correct. (Also, a real-life example from one of my students.)

With the adept statement, you get the sense of a solid career, but leave open the possibility of increased expenses sapping away the increased income. This happens all the time—you get a boon with Magic, and suddenly the HVAC needs to be replaced, which eats up all the money you made.

The master statement opens the door for all kinds of income streams and opportunities as well as a career, but clarifies steady flow rather than a one-time boon. You also frame the numbers in terms of what's left over rather than what you take in, which helps eliminate the potential for emergencies and new expenses tapping the new income.

Future or Present Tense?

There are a lot of people out there who advocate the practice of framing statements of intent to reflect whatever is desired in the present tense, as if it has already happened. An example would be "I have a fulfilling love life with a wonderful partner" as opposed to "Bring me a lover that will fulfill and excite me." The idea is that by saying it has already happened, you sure it up in the mind and make it more concrete.

This practice is widespread and I did it for decades myself, starting back in the 1980s when I read the *Necronomicon Spellbook*, in which Simon advised holding your goal as having already occurred in the mind. As far as I can tell, the practice made its way into Magical work from the New Thought movement, the same movement that eventually gave birth to "The Secret." There is nothing wrong with this, and if you are doing a purely mental type of Magic, it makes perfect sense. Most Sorcery, however, is not purely mental, and you might be shocked how little your thoughts and beliefs have to do with it.

As the concepts behind the Strategic Sorcery approach came into focus, I stopped forming declarations like this and now actively teach against forming statements in the present tense, or spending too much time visualizing things as if they already happened. There are a few reasons why I don't like this approach.

I have found that the best approach to Sorcery relies upon figuring out the most cunning steps to achieve your goal, then enchanting each of those steps along the way. Using the example of a job spell, you may do one large spell at the beginning that uses a basic statement of intent to find work, such as the examples we gave previously. But that's not the end of your Magic. You will want to start networking and perhaps invoke Mercury or other powers to bring you in touch with the right people. You will want to enchant your resume so that it attracts attention. When you get a job interview, you will want to do some influencing and glamour Magic to make yourself memorable and ensure a good impression. You may also want to do some Magic so that everything is timed well at each stage. This will be explored more fully in Key 10.

If we make a statement of intent that suggests we already have gotten the job, it doesn't leave room to focus on the rest of the strategy. In other words, focusing on the goal as being already achieved leaves open the chance that you will skimp or skip on other the steps needed to get there.

Telling yourself that you have already won your prize makes you *feel* good, but it does little to get you toward your goal. In fact, often people mistake this feeling of success with success itself. Recent research into the effects of positive thinking have affirmed my observations.[1] One study showed that participants who were made to feel parched and who visualized themselves drinking a cool glass of water were less motivated to get up and quench their real thirst with real water. In study after study, research shows that visualizing yourself as having achieved something already makes you less motivated to go out and achieve it. On the one hand, it shows the power of the mind, but like all power, unless it is applied wisely, it becomes a source of trouble.

Even in creative visualization and purely mental Magic, I prefer a contrasting technique that does involve visualizing a desired outcome, but follows it up with visualizations or affirmations of the path that will lead to it, obstacles that you may encounter, and what you will do when you hit those obstacles. You start at your goal and work backward to the present, then forward again in great detail. I learned this trick, oddly enough, not from a Magician but from an interview with Frank Lucas, the notorious drug kingpin who was the subject of the book and movie *American Gangster*. He would shut himself up for a week and do this careful visualization in great detail before embarking on a big venture.

The other reason not to form statements in the present tense is that what you want to occur really hasn't happened yet, and you *know* that. Magic is a subtle art that defies and skirts what people consider real. Because of this, I try to engage in as little fantasy as possible around it and instead focus on the details of what needs to be done and how Sorcery can help you achieve it.

Caveats and Modifiers

Apart from stating what we want to happen, the statement of intent often includes what we *don't* want to happen. Unless you are a sociopath, I am sure that you don't want Aunt Ruth to kick the bucket just so you can get this month's rent together with her inheritance. This old nugget is an unlikely scenario but technically a possible one, and so we try to limit harm through caveats and modifiers.

Like so many things in the world of people who practice Magic, it is hard to find anyone with a reasonable middle of the road position. Folks seem to either advocate doing whatever it takes to get what they want regardless of the consequences or are so deeply concerned that they may inadvertently inconvenience someone or unfairly advantage themselves that they never actually do any effective Magic. I am deeply saddened by the folks who find it acceptable to throw down serious curses at their ex or their boss, but there is little that I can say that will dissuade them. This section is for those who want to walk a sensible road where they get things done, while making reasonable steps to manage the impact of their Magic.

By far, the most popular caveat to Magical statements of intent is "as long as it harms no one"—which seems, at first, to be a convenient and straightforward way to be nice and ethical. The only problem is that almost everything harms *someone somehow.* This isn't a feature of Magical action, it's a feature of action itself. That job you want? Someone else wants it to. If you get it, they don't. Same with the lover you want or the house you are trying to get. The court case you are trying to win will also generate a loser. That's the way the world works. This is why I often remind my students that **"All Sorcery has a body count."** Maybe body count is a little strong, but it's a way to keep the repercussions of your actions in focus. You cannot exist, much less act, in this world without it affecting other people. This is why Victor Anderson, the founder of the Feri Tradition of Witchcraft, once said, "Poetry is white Magic. Black Magic is anything that works."

One of the first money spells I ever did resulted in me finding the near-exact amount in a wallet that fell out of someone's pocket under a roller coaster. The spell worked, but some other guy would have been out $50 if I had not returned the wallet, which I did. I have done protection spells that resulted in the person I was protecting someone from getting sick and being hospitalized. Although I don't do this kind of work, I have a student who is very good at targeted love Magic for clients, and has left behind of trail of broken hearts from competing suitors who did *not* have her Magic in their corner.

Unfortunately, because Magic is not within the scope of what many people think of as ordinary action, people overthink it and place all kinds of caveats to prevent unintended harm. The problem is that by asking for zero harm, we are lowering our chances of success, not raising them. It is worse than doing nothing at all, because by doing a spell that prevents us from harming anyone else, you are almost guaranteed *not* to get that promotion!

You get it? Your Magic is reaching into reality to tweak it, and if you state at the outset that no matter what the spell says, it should not harm anyone, you are likely to sabotage yourself in situations where your success means someone else's failure.

So am I saying never use a caveat or modifier? No. I am just suggesting you be smart and reasonable. Realize that the more caveats you place on how something works, the more reduced are the avenues of influence you have at your disposal, causing your chance for success diminish correspondingly. As I said, unless you are a sociopath or simply do not believe that Magic is real, most issues you come across do not have a "by any means necessary" price tag on them, so asking that no one be killed or maimed is fine.

Just try to use the caveats and modifiers with care, and keep in mind your actions affect others. Put this into perspective. A good rule of thumb is: If it's something you would feel okay about doing without Magic, it is probably something worth doing with Magic as well.

The Take-Away

The problem this key addresses, put bluntly, is people aiming great spells at stupid stuff. If we put as much care into our Statements of Intent as we do into our spells, this wouldn't happen. This key is related to Key 2: Stop Making Crappy Goals. To use a firearms analogy, the goal is your target and the spell is your cannon, the statement of intent then is your aim. Be a marksman. Be precise and clever and do your best to limit collateral damage while still hitting your target.

In Key 2, Harold enchanted for wealth and was unhappy with his 10 bucks. He probably followed that up with a more specific spell to gain more money from his job, which of course resulted in more hours at work. This is a real-life example, and there are dozens of field reports in the Strategic Sorcery archives of people complaining like this when they get exactly what they asked for. Being more skillful is the key. Some of the later keys address this problem as well, so if you have ever found yourself overworked as the result of your requests for increased wealth, pay attention.

Key 7:
Emergency Magic
Is Bad Magic

Have you ever heard someone say something like "Magic should be a last resort, only to be used in dire emergencies?" Me too. It's one of the worst pieces of advice I have ever gotten, and dispelling this tired nugget of folly it is our 7th Key.

Magic is a skill just like any other. It can certainly be helpful in an emergency, but if you *only* use it in emergencies, how skillful do you think your Magic will be? Not very. That's why, rather than reserve Sorcery for emergencies, I weave it into everything I do. My life plans include Sorcery from the get-go.

I understand why teachers tell people that Magic should be reserved for emergencies. You don't want to give the impression that all of life's problems can be handled with spells instead of mundane efforts. I have seen the kinds of extreme Magical lengths people will go to in order to avoid a relatively simple solution that just requires a little non-Magical work. I get it, but it sets up a false dichotomy where there are mundane or "real world" solutions versus Magical solutions. If we understand the first key, that Magic is an influence, we will have no trouble understanding that mundane and Magical efforts work best together, and as such, there is no need to reserve Magic for emergencies.

Some Witches and Magicians consider Magic a super-natural event, and therefore something that must be engaged in only occasionally. I disagree and consider Magic part of the natural world, one that is simply not fully understood by science yet.

Others see Magic as an unfair advantage, or dangerously powerful. These are the people who will not use Magic to do well on a job interview or date, for fear of "over-riding someone else's free will." Let me assure you that, though the occasional miracle or shocking result happens, and extreme modes of Magic exist, most Magic is simply an influence. Is it an unfair advantage? Maybe, but don't we all have different advantages? Is it fair that some people look like Jon Hamm or Halle Berry? Is it fair that some people have family connections?

Look around at the Pagan and Occult communities. Do we seem like people who are dripping in unfair advantage? The world is not fair. Get over it and use what you have.

The Power of Proactive Sorcery

When I first coined the phrase "emergency Magic is bad Magic," it got repeated a lot, and like most things that get repeated a lot, it was misunderstood. I don't mean that Magic is bad to use in emergencies—Magic can absolutely help you out in an emergency. I also don't mean that you are doing something wrong if you have an emergency; we all occasionally have emergencies from time to time.

My reason for saying that "emergency Magic is bad Magic" is that proactive Magic helps keep emergencies at bay. Because we study Sorcery, Witchcraft, and Magic, those will be among the tools best able to help us. They give us an advantage, so why *wouldn't* we use them? By using Jupiterian powers to make sure our business grows at a steady pace, we avoid the frantic petitions to demons when we are about to go under. If we make offerings and sweetening spells to make sure that our work at our job is well received by our bosses, we never have to use the binding spells on them to keep from getting fired. If we invoke to help us understand and grow closer to our partners, we may never have to use the court case Magic to make out well in the divorce settlement. If we use divination to help us avoid bad investments and ask Baphomet to help them grow, we may well avoid having to do the panicky money drawing that so often doesn't really help in the long run.

Emergency Magic Is Often Too Late

A few years ago, I was called in by a couple shop owners to help turn the downward slide of their store around. They had been floundering for over a year, and when I asked what kind of Magic they had done thus far, they replied they did not do anything because they were taught to only use Magic for dire emergencies, and now that they were officially in a dire emergency they contacted me.

I did some readings that indicated Tzadkiel, the Archangel of Jupiter, would be a suitable power to provide the help they needed. I did a cleansing on the store, set up talismans for success, and invoked Tzadkiel to bless the operation and bring victory. The result was that the next morning, Tzadkiel appeared to one of the shop owners, not in a dream but in the blank television screen, and asked her to move the store to a different location—which they did. Business improved but only slightly, and there was still not enough money to rotate stock. Tzadkiel's efforts looked like a bust, until someone came into the shop and asked to buy it. This person owned a small regional chain and was looking to expand.

Was the operation a failure? Certainly, we did not save the shop, and that was a letdown. We only marginally made it more successful—just enough to make it interesting to a buyer that would save my friends from going deep into debt from the venture. It was the best that could be arrived at given the circumstances. Had we done a similar spell earlier, we might have had a better result. Had Tzadkiel been invoked as patron of the business at the start, and Magic been incorporated into the launch and subsequent operation, things might have turned out different.

The moral of the story is that by the time you are in an emergency, it is usually too late for a great outcome. Often the best that can be arrived at is minimizing harm. If you are waiting until the shit hits the fan before you break out the bell book and candle, don't expect rousing success.

Sometimes a Good Emergency Is Just What We Need

This is a tough lesson to learn, but sometimes what we perceive as an emergency is just what we need to grow. Early in my Magical career, someone very dear to me robbed a bank and was very likely going to prison. His family asked if I could do any Magic on the court case to stop this, but I refused. I refused because the reason this person robbed the bank was to repay drug dealers, and it was just an escalation of the staggeringly bad decisions he had been making for his entire adult life. While I am no fan of the American prison system and have little faith in its rehabilitative potential, I divined that this was in fact the best thing that could happen to him at this time.

I was right. After prison, my friend went on to lead a productive life, get married, and be much loved by many people. He passed recently from cancer, surrounded by loved ones rather than getting killed through underworld mishaps. His emergency was necessary for better options to emerge.

Recently, a regular client contacted me because he feared his partners were going to buy him out of his firm. I reminded him that he has been telling me every month how unhappy he is there, and how he wants to work on a different type of law if only he had the time to devote. Now he will, so it is likely a good thing, but it still feels like a disaster because it threatens his sense of comfort.

We will deal with this concept more fully in the 18th Key, but some emergencies just need to happen. People value comfort above uncertainty, even when that comfort is holding them back from progress. But often when looking back on life, it was these rejections and disasters that cleared the way for a better life. The problem is that as wielders of spells, we can forestall these emergencies from happening. You may think the dangers of Magic lie in offended spirits and wrathful demons, but the greater danger by far is the ability to cast spells that trap us in the job we hate and married to the person we can't stand anymore. All in the name of comfort.

The arms of Baphomet read "solve" and "coagula," dissolution and rebuilding. This is a process that is rarely comfortable, but it is how progress is made and how Magicians are made great.

The Take-Away

In our comic for this key, Harold is in danger of losing his day job, the one he complained worked him too hard in the previous key. If he had done some Magic to improve his job, he wouldn't be in this mess. Losing the job is probably exactly what he needs though. We will explore this further in the 18th Key.

The problem that this key seeks to address is the one of Sorcery only being applied to fix problems that arise rather than incorporated as part of our plans from the start. If Magic is so much a part of your life that you call yourself a Witch, a Magician, a Sorcerer, or Sorceress, why wouldn't you incorporate this into your plans? This is your passion, your interest, and hopefully your skillful advantage. Use it!

PART 2:
EXECUTION

ENSURING THAT YOUR WORKINGS WORK

Key 8:
Embrace the Power
of Offerings

If you asked my students what the single greatest game-changer for improving their Magic that they got from my teachings, most of them would say "offerings." A lot of you reading this might already be well acquainted with offerings to spirits; some of you are surely initiated into Vodou, Candomble, or another African traditional religion where offerings play a huge role.

That is where I first encountered them myself. The first offering I ever did was to Papa Legba shortly after moving to Philadelphia, in hopes that he would help me gather a group of Magicians to work with. The morning after one of the biggest snowstorms that decade, I went out to the corner of 6th and Pine, the corner where my apartment was located, and drew a very large veve of Legba that extended one-fourth of the way up each street on that block. I made an offering of a coconut filled with palm oil, and a candle, and asked for his help. I want to be clear here: This is not how proper Vodou is done. This was a much younger me, and what I knew of Vodou came from Milo Rigaud's book, some correspondence with Max Beauvoir, and Louis Martine's Tarot. Thankfully the Lwa sometimes smile on fools, and later that week, a friend contacted me and asked if I was interested in starting a Philadelphia OTO group. One month after that offering, the first meeting happened at my apartment. That group pulled me into contact with some of the best people I have ever worked with. Though I am no longer a member of the OTO, I still occasionally get asked to teach there, and am very proud that Thelesis Oasis, a small group that started in my living room, still exists 20 years later.

Gumball Magic

This type of Magic—making an offering to a specific spirit for a specific service, is common throughout the world. It is what my friend Persephone calls "gumball Magic": Put a quarter in the machine, get a gumball out—that simple. If you know what a spirit likes, or what is traditionally offered, then you can make an offering and ask for a boon in return.

The offerings not only honor and in some cases feed the spirit, but act as a foothold into the physical world and are yet another way of bridging that divide between the spiritual and the material.

Sometimes the offering is part of the spell itself, and you do something like feed a spirit hot foods or herbs to "heat it up" and get it to act quickly. Other offerings can cool it down, helpful when cooler heads need to prevail.

Whatever spirit you are working with, the offerings will require some research on your part. Both as individuals and as classes of spirits, there are different things that are appreciated, and others that are taboo. Tobacco may be appreciated by most of the spirits from the Diasporic religions of the Caribbean, but are repugnant to some Dharmapalas of Tibet, who legend says helped Padmasambhava remove the plant from the country in the 8th century. Burnt meat was appreciated by Jehovah as well as wrathful spirits the world over, but the Nagas are so repelled by the eating of animals that some of their Puja ceremonies require the person making the offering to abstain from meat and even eggs for 24 hours prior.

If you want to make an offering to a specific spirit, start with the living tradition if one exists. Then go to the folklore and history for examples of what may be appropriate. Sometimes you will find offerings that you can make easily enough such as eggs, dandelions, and honey to Hekate. Other times you will come across offerings that are unmanageable or ethically questionable, such as 100 oxen to Hekate, which, while traditional, is hard to pull off in the backyard. After your research, you can use divination to fill in gaps and confirm your ideas. The final test will be whether the deity takes your offering and fulfills your request.

Of course, there are other deeper approaches than the tit-for-tat gumball Magic where you make an offering in exchange for a service. A regular practice of offerings will help you build real relationships.

Regular Offerings

If you make offerings a part of your regular practice, then you will develop more powerful and long-term associations with the spirits than you can with simple contracts. One of my Haitian teachers stressed this as a difference between the Bokor (Sorcerer for hire) and Houngan or Mambo (Priest or Priestess of Vodou) in Haiti. When I began to study Tibetan Magic, offerings were again emphasized in an even more advanced and profound mode. In this case, offerings were not only done to spirits that we were working with through the tradition, but were made on a regular basis to large classes of beings that inhabit the whole world. This helped up my Sorcery success rate dramatically.

Think of it this way: If you asked a stranger to loan you 50 dollars, they would probably say no. If you asked someone you worked with for 50 bucks, they may lend it or they may not, depending upon your experience with that person. If you asked your best friend for 50 dollars, it's almost certain that they would lend it if they had it and ask if you needed anything else. They would also probably not be concerned about the date of payback because you have a long history, likely making gestures of goodwill to one another for many years. These gestures of goodwill are offerings, and making them regularly will put the whole universe just a bit more in your corner when you need something.

I follow a pattern of offerings inspired by Tibetan Magic during which I burn incense (which flows upward) and pour water, tea, or whiskey to the ground each morning (flowing downward), all the while acknowledging four classes of recipients.

The first and highest classification of guest are the deities as well as those beings that can be considered enlightened such as Buddhas, ascended masters, and if you like, the universe itself. This type of guest doesn't in any way *need* the offerings that we make; the benefit is strictly ours. By making offerings to such beings, we remind ourselves what we constantly strive toward, and in turn build a connection to beings that have achieved that level of realization. It is an exchange of energy like that between a parent and child. Your child may give you something that you neither want nor need, but you not only accept it, but go out of your way to enjoy it fully, because you know that it cultivates certain qualities in the child. In a similar way, we can say that the Gods do not need our offerings, but that doesn't mean we don't need to make them.

The second classification of guest are the protectors, guardians, Saints, and lesser deities of a tradition. These are beings of great power but who are not fully realized beings. They do enjoy the substance of the offering that is made, but do not depend upon them.

The third classification is simply all regular beings. This can include all nonphysical entities such as nature spirits and ghosts, as well as the spirits of all currently incarnated beings. In short, everyone, but most especially those beings in your local area—the woods near your house, the lake or ocean nearby, the trees in your yard, the winds that blow through. The spirits on the land and all that is upon it.

The fourth classification singles out beings to whom you owe debt. This debt could be problems that come from this life or a previous life. It may have to do with specific ways that you have dealt with Magic or just how you live your life. The most common example is a spirit of nature that you have run afoul of through your ordinary human actions, like driving through a certain area or dumping trash. A good portion of the traditional shaman's work was keeping the balance between our world and the world of the spirits, a role that the Sorcerer will sometimes be asked to fulfill. Being a Magician, you are even more able to trample upon the turf of spirits or powers that you may not even be aware of. Making offerings to this class of beings can act as a type of uncrossing that can, by itself, make life start to run more smoothly.

Types of Offering

It's true that the real substance of an offering is in spiritual substance, not gross physical matter, but the use of physical offerings is a good way to materialize your result. A good physical offering draws the spirit and powers a bit further into our realm and gives them more of a connection to our lives. The physical offering is also more pleasing to those beings whose presence reaches into the etheric level such as ghosts and some nature spirits. So, although some people want to visualize offerings or make only the barest of visible efforts, an actual physical offering should be present as a basis, even if it is then multiplied through visualization.

Some examples of offerings include:

- ⊛ **Incense:** The ascending smoke is not only said to carry one's prayers to the higher realms, but to be literally consumed by classes of beings called "scent eaters."

- ⊛ **Light:** A nearly universal symbol for wisdom, light is appreciated by most spiritual beings and is thought to be literally consumed by certain beings. Whatever you use as an offering should be separate from your work lights, the lights you use to illuminate your temple.

- ⊛ **Water:** Symbolizing purity and washing clean. Water is an extremely attractive and calming substance for many spirits to linger near, especially spirits of the dead.

- ⊛ **Fruit:** Symbolizes the fruit of Gnosis and the surrender of something valuable of yours to the spirits.

- ⊛ **Flowers:** A symbol of beauty and impermanence, some spirits absorb their beauty, some their scent, and still others value their very impermanence.

- ⊛ **Meat:** Valued most by strong, wild, and wrathful spirits, meat is a potent offering. It was the smell of the burning flesh that was offered to YHVH in the Bible, and is still a powerful incense today. Already prepared or even raw meat can also be offered to beings that like that kind of thing.

- ⊛ **Money:** Money is enjoyed by spirits of departed humans and by certain beings of the second classification that value your sacrifice. It can be also a powerful offering to those beings who govern money matters, but its offering must be handled properly. In some cases, burning of money as an offering to the spirits of the dead might be appreciated, which is why you see "hell notes" for sale in Chinatown often. At other times, this might be considered offensive to the spirits of money itself.

✦ **Symbols:** Certain beings have various symbols and tools that they are associated with. Love Goddesses seem to enjoy perfume and sometimes even sex toys, war deities love swords and even guns, and wealth spirits love hoarding jewels and money. Spirits of dead Magicians seem to like talismans and Occult bric-a-brac. Use your knowledge and intuition to choose.

✦ **Charitable donations:** There are small sacrifices that you can make that can be used as offerings. Money and personal objects are also a way to give of one's self, but be sure that you are ready to let whatever it is go. Your own blood is an excellent offering to some spirits, as is the pain that is re-leased when you draw it. Pain itself can be offered to spirits. I have worked with Magic involving BDSM at times in the past, and have made an offering of the pain from whipping a willing submissive as a sort of "human sacrifice."

✦ **Animal sacrifice:** Obviously animal sacrifices are a common offering to the spirits both throughout history and in many religions throughout the world. I don't do them or encour-age them, and certainly don't advocate for them to anyone who is not in a tradition where they are already done. With training, context, and skill, it can be a moving and sacred gesture to spirits and Gods that appreciate that kind of offer-ing. Done without skill, it is an unholy travesty. My rule of thumb is that if you grew up killing your own meat and can do it quickly with little pain, then it's not such a huge jump to include animal sacrifice in your rites—especially if you are in a tradition that already practices it. If you are doing it because it's forbidden or somehow "dark" in your mind, then skip it, please. To people who live a little closer to their food source than the local supermarket, animal sacrifice is no "darker" than getting supper ready.

Disposing of Offerings

If you do choose to make an offering other than incense or a libation poured into the ground, you will be quickly confronted with a problem: What do you do with the offerings afterward?

The answer is a little complicated and depends upon what you are offering and whether you are making the offerings at a permanent shrine in your own home or making a temporary offering at a crossroads or something like that.

In the case of offering food, flowers, or anything that spoils in your own home, you should keep it there as long as it's not stinking up the place, attracting bugs, or looking shabby. Those familiar with Tantra might point out stories of Mahasiddhas making rancid offerings to reveal the inherent purity of all things. That's okay if you are a Mahasiddha, but if you can't fly or make imprints of your hand just by touching solid stone, then do yourself and the spirits a favor and stick to nicer presentations, unless a spirit specifically asks for something gross.

When disposing of food offerings, I do not throw it in the rubbish with common waste. Instead I try to find a place in the woods or on the side of the road to leave it. If you are making a food offering in the wild, then the problem gets handled for you; whether its animals in the forest or homeless people in the city, you can consider that the guests consume the best part and leave the rest.

In the case of objects like mojo bags, jewelry, bottles of perfume, and so on, or other permanent objects like money, the rule is to leave it be. If you are leaving money or another object in public, don't worry about what happens to it; just let it go and don't look back. In the case of a shrine or altar in your own home, you should only offer those things that you are prepared to leave permanently. Every now and then, someone will get so addicted to making physical offerings (and thus train the spirits they work with to expect them) that their living space becomes overcrowded. Don't let this happen to you. Make offerings of energy and astral objects all you want, and certainly things like incense, light, and libations should be regular if not daily, but leave the permanent physical offerings for special occasions.

Whatever you do, do not take the offerings back. If you offer money, that money is no longer yours. Do not ever spend it. If you offer whiskey, don't consume it as part of the offering. You can consume it along with the spirits, but not their portion, unless that is what the tradition calls for, and it sometimes does.

Also know that spirits do not always relate to size the way that we do. Often a small dagger, or even a toy-sized sword will suffice as an offering to a martial being. Just a couple dimes or even pennies will be just as enjoyable to spirits as larger sums. Leaving hundreds of dollars on an altar is just foolish and pleases no one. Donate some money in the name of the being you wish to please, just don't let that amount of money go to waste.

A Daily Spirit Feast

The following is a short general-purpose offering that I use on a regular basis. It has three parts: Purification of Offerings, Inviting the Guests, Making Offerings, and License to Depart. Spoken parts are in **bold**.

PURIFICATION OF OFFERINGS

Gather some incense. I recommend juniper, myrrh, and frankincense, or Tibetan Riwo Sang Cho as an all-purpose incense, but you can alter this as you need. You will also want some liquid such as tea or water as a libation for daytime offerings. Nighttime offerings should have light and whiskey or another alcohol.

Sound the word **ISTUM** and imagine the offerings on fire. You can pore breathe fire if you have time, but it is not necessary if you are in a hurry. Sound the word **ANNA** and imagine a gust of air blowing out of the fire. Sound the word **NINA** and imagine that a flow of water emanates from you and washes the offering.

INVITING THE GUESTS

Category One

To the Gods and Goddesses, angels and avatars, most especially to [name your most important patrons and divine beings that you wish to acknowledge by name]*, and to the overseeing powers of this land on which I dwell, I give offerings of respect.*

Category Two

To my ancestors, protectors, and allies, I give thanks and offerings, most especially to [name your most important ancestors, protectors, and spirit allies that you wish to acknowledge by name]*, I give offerings of gratitude.*

Category Three

To all beings of the sky, the land, the underworld; to all sentient beings in all the ten directions and three times, most especially those who dwell in the area upon, above, and under the earth, I give offerings of substance and nourishment.

Category Four

To all beings to whom I owe a debt, and who I have angered by mistaken or ignorant action, I give offerings of supplication and pacification.

MAKING OFFERINGS

Make the gesture of offering, flourish your incense, pour your libation on the ground, hold aloft your light, set out your cups of alcohol. Do whatever you do as a signature of offering—truth be told, it doesn't matter. It's a signal to the spirits that the offering is made. Add in your own visualization of the offerings multiplying and filling all space. Spend some time actually looking at what the spirits do with the clouds and how they manifest.

Nadan ma-qlu—enjoy the offerings. Ela ma-qlu—be pleased and fulfilled.

LICENSE TO DEPART

Put in your own license here, or don't and just let it hang. If I am doing the offering indoors, I always do one; if not, I often let it hang. When you leave, bow in respect just as you would if you left a party.

A Word of Warning

As with any advice, there is a word of warning—three, in fact:

1. Do not offer the finest and most expensive things to the spirits. Save those for times when you need special help. Just like a date, if you start off with very expensive restaurants, that is what becomes the norm, and you go broke. Save the Johnny Walker Blue for when you need the big promotion. As a day to day, the Johnny Walker Black will do just fine.

2. Making offerings to pacify spirits that can be pacified with offerings is wonderful. That does not mean all spirits that are upset or causing problems can be pacified thusly. You may need protection and exorcism from time to time.

3. If you have the ability to communicate with spirits, either directly or through a medium like a spirit board or pendulum, you may get asked for bigger and more elaborate offerings. It is okay to say no. See Key 21 for more on this.

The Take-Away

The problem that this key seeks to solve is one of relationships with spirits and the world around us. Some traditions spend a lot of time on offerings but many of us who come from a Ceremonial Magic, Wiccan, or other type of Western background have been neglecting this important tool. Offerings get things done, and even broad offerings to the world at large can grease the wheels of your Sorcery. In this key's comic, Harold has been making a lot of demands on Salphegor, but hasn't made any offerings yet. Maybe if he spent some time making offerings, things would go a bit better for him.

The ritual here given as an example is something you can institute daily or weekly, and is meant as a regular practice. If there is a specific spirit or class of spirits who likes something special, then do the research and make sure that you are not serving something that they don't like. Keep in mind, though, that you will find conflicting approaches and rationales even within the same tradition. The world is not neat and tidy, and the world of the spirits is even less so.

Key 9:
DIY Is Over-Rated

You have heard it many times: There is Magic in the act of creation. You hear it a lot because it's true. Lovingly crafting a tool, an image, or an invocation is a Magical act that changes the creator as much as it does the base materials he is creating with. A long time ago, a teacher told me that the value of making something yourself cannot be overstated. Therein lies the problem—I think the value of doing it yourself *can* be overstated and often is. Maybe you have heard one of these nuggets:

> "Nothing will *ever* have the power of a tool that you make yourself."

> "Tradition is fine, but *never* **as good as your own beliefs and rituals.**"

> "Write your own rituals; they will *always* **be more potent than anything you read in a book.**"

This sounds really neat and appeals to the go-my-own-way streak that brought many of us to Magic in the first place. It also appeals to the lazy, I-don't-feel-like-studying part of ourselves. The problem is that ideas like these fail to take into account anything other than the power of creation. What about the power that a skilled craftsman brings? What about the power of time-honored rites? Doing something yourself can be wonderful, but doing *everything* yourself, and doing it well, is impossible.

The Power of Tradition

Recently a student wanted to start doing St. Cyprian work. I asked what prayers she would be using, and she said that she wanted to write her own because it would be more powerful and personal that way. The problem is that she had never done work with Cyprian before and had only heard about him recently because of all the press he has been getting in the Occult world. Why wouldn't you avail yourself of the many prayers and novenas that already exist? By all means, I think there is power in writing one of your own—I even put one together myself—but why wouldn't you try out one or more of the traditional approaches first, so that you could at least get to know what they are about? It's kind of like writing a sonnet about someone that you have never met.

Furthermore, when you think about it, it's more than a little disrespectful. I think of traditional methods for contacting spirits similar to established approaches for contacting people. If someone completely ignores the protocols I have set up for contacting me, and instead shows up at my house, I will refuse to talk to them. Some spirits take this view as well. Before writing any rites to Hekate, Padmasambhava, Cyprian, Jupiter, or any other being I work with, I try to avail myself of methods that have already been established and then go from there. It's polite and grants a better understanding than if you just wing it.

And you know what? Even after I write my own stuff, I *still* use those other methods quite often. There is a power in creation, but there is a power in tradition as well. These two, creation and tradition, feed off each other. Creation divorced from tradition quickly degenerates into wild fantasy or reinventing the wheel. Tradition divorced from creativity can lead to dead rites that no longer serve.

The Power of Craftsmanship

It is impossible to be good at everything, so why expect that you can do everything yourself? When someone like Frater Ashen Chassan creates a tool or Aidan Watcher creates a talisman, it is a masterful and beautiful thing to behold. Their work inspires faith and awe, not only because they are first-rate Magicians, but expert craftsmen.

Now one could argue that anyone can become a master craftsman with effort and just a little talent, and that may be true, but if that is not your calling, you probably won't want to invest that time. DIY purists will insist that any attempt, even one that winds up looking like a kindergartener's art project, will be better than something someone else has done. I say poppycock! Craftsmanship has value, easily as much or more than doing it yourself. I have old tools that I made in high school, but I never use them because, frankly, they look like crap. I would rather purchase or commission something nice and consecrate it to the work. In this case, the consecration is my contribution to the creation.

In any given skill, there are those who gain competency, others who seek mastery, and still others who seek perfection. Perfection is, of course, a lifetime dedication and there will only be one or rarely two things in your life that you devote that level of dedication to. Mastery is time-consuming in terms of thousands of hours over many years. You can master a few things in this life, but not everything. Competency in most things can be gained with just a small investment of time and effort. If all you need is competency, then that's fine. But why not take advantage of masters in the field?

Learning from Something Doesn't Mean You Have to Keep Doing It

When I was young, I learned the basics of making oils, baths, and powders from a few gracious teachers. When I took cat yronwood's Hoodoo course back in the early 2000s (I am graduate #99), I learned even more and made several oils to make sure I understood the principals and Magic involved. Later, when I first was learning about Alchemy, I managed to extract Sal Salis from wood in a very time-consuming but transformative process. Some things I learned can *only* be learned by making it myself. Some things can only be learned by devising a formula from scratch. The value of these lessons is immense, but does that mean I have to do it myself forever?

I don't *enjoy* fannying about with herbs and oils. I love anointing with oils in Magic, but I hate mixing them and getting excessively involved in the creation of things that can be done just as, or more, effectively by others. In fact, I pretty much avoid as much arts and crafts as possible so that I have time to actually *do* the Magic.

In short, I learned how to do it. I do it when I have to. I don't when I don't have to. Far from suffering, my Magic is often more effective by relying on people who are masters of their craft.

If Everything Reflects Who and What You Already Are, There Is No Growth

A lot of people start out their spiritual and Magical lives by rejecting anything that does not reflect themselves. They create their own traditions of Witchcraft and Magic because no tradition out there will "reflect my beliefs like one I make myself." The problem with this is that traditions don't exist to reflect what you already believe. They exist to give you a framework to grow within. You don't need traditions to tell you that you're right. You need them to challenge you with the possibility that you might be wrong.

Traditions exist to give many people who all have slightly different beliefs a framework to come together. This is true of rituals as well. I *hate* some of William Gray's overly alliterative writing style, but I do it when I meet with my Sodality because it is something that we can all use and has become a tradition with its own potency. It is an opportunity to grow within a tradition and have a common ground for work with peers, rather than something that must reflect my style and preferences.

The act of creation is an important and potent Magical act, but when you feel like you must create everything to be a reflection of your own beliefs and style, you are building yourself a cage out of mirrors. What begins as self-exploration can quickly devolve into solipsism if gone unchecked.

When DIY Is the Magic

Now, that I have spent a key arguing that you can buy oils instead of making them and perform other people's rituals rather than doing everything yourself, let me take a moment to point out that in some cases DIY *is* the Magic. If, for instance, one were a traditional Witch devoted to Tubal Cain, the first blacksmith, it would be an incredible act of devotion to learn traditional blacksmithing—to have a forge, to work the iron, to present new creations into the world, each as an offering to Old Cain. This is a powerful thing and the thing that you will be perfecting your whole life. Your soul would be heated, reshaped, and cooled along with the metal, just as the Alchemist is transformed by the making of the Elixir.

You cannot play at this or go in halfway. You have to commit serious time, money, and effort, which means that there are other things you won't be doing. You cannot do everything. Thoreau once said, "The price of anything is the amount of life you exchange for it." I hope this key convinces you of the worth of mastering a few things in this life, and valuing the things that other people have mastered, rather than feel like you must do everything yourself.

The Take-Away

Harold is trying to command Salphegor with a Lunar Wand that he made from an old crescent wrench. Sal's not buying it. Clearly Harold is not a master craftsman when it comes to wand-making. The problem this key addresses is the impossible task of having to do everything yourself. The solution is to question whether this is even necessary. Ask yourself the following questions:

1. **Is there something to learn here by doing it myself?** For example, I have internalized lessons from drawing the Heptameron Circle on the ground that I think could not be gotten any other way.

2. **Once I have learned that lesson, do I have to keep doing it myself?** I did it, and now I have the circle drawn in paint on a drop cloth. I can fill the names in with other pieces of cloth as the season changes. I don't feel like I need to keep doing it myself every time.

3. **Is it a lesson I need to learn?** We don't have time to learn every individual lesson. There are mysteries involved in the creation of dud-tsi pills that I will probably never know because those mysteries are primarily for people who are called to that work. That doesn't stop me from using the pills as part of my Tantric work.

4. **Is this something I love to do and have the time and desire to master?** I love writing and experimenting with ritual, and I devote the time to doing it. I love to work with wood and have made many wands, but no longer have the time to devote to it, so I don't anymore. I have never liked mixing oils, and while I learned how to do it reasonably well, I still tend to avoid it.

5. **Is there someone else who makes it better than I can?** If someone else made a really nice version of the circle, maybe with organic paints that have fluid condensers mixed in, I would not hesitate to buy it and use it. My hazel wand recently broke, and I am probably going to buy one from Jake Stratton Kent for some upcoming work with the Verum, rather than make another one myself. I will reconsecrate it of course, but I trust that he cut them at the right time and place.

DIY is great but don't let it stop you from taking advantage of the works of other artists and craftsmen, engaging in traditions that you might learn and grow from, or just save a you little time that you could spend enjoying your life.

Key 10:
Use Macro- and
Micro-Enchantment

In late 2000, I was looking for a job. I had just spent several months in Nepal and so had a huge gap in my resume. Before I went to Nepal, I was an "underwriter technician" (aka glorified administrative assistant) for a large insurance company. I dropped college after two years and had no degree. This is not at all uncommon for people in the Occult and pagan worlds: a focus on the mystical sometimes comes at the expense of advancement in career and traditional education. It was also even more common in the 1990s, the decade that practically celebrated the Gen-X slacker. The only problem is that I was tired of slacking. I wanted a job, one with benefits and weekends off.

I wanted to come back to the United States and embrace the life of a productive grown-up. I set up an altar to my favorite Buddhist God of increase and wealth: Dzambhala. I would say his mantra every day and, as is traditional, I would offer water by pouring it over his statue as an offering. This offering comes from a legend that claims that Dzambhala stepped in the way of a rock thrown at the Buddha, taking the hit. The Buddha healed him and told Dzambhala that in the future, anyone who calls upon him and pours water on his head to soothe him should be granted both material and spiritual wealth. As I poured the water, I asked Dzambhala to bring me a new job, one that would pay me better than I had ever been paid. One that would give me the perks I wanted. One that I was probably not qualified for in the least.

A week or so after beginning Dzambhala practice, a close friend told me about a position that would ordinarily require a four-year degree or years of experience in the field. At very least, I should have a lot of tele-command internet knowledge that I didn't have. He offered to work with me to get me up to speed. I did a spell invoking Manjushri, the Buddha of intelligence, to help me qualify for the job and absorb information easily. I did 10,000 mantras in one sitting while breathing the power into a sesame seed, then ate the seed to allow his power to grow within me. The day of the interview, I did a Kurukulla ritual to help charm the person who would be interviewing me. I got the job and started a new career in VOIP telephony.

What Is Macro- and Micro-Enchantment?

Macro-enchantment is a single ritual designed to get you the thing you want—a job, a love, a win, whatever. It is the only ritual that most people do, a spell to solve for X.

Micro-enchantments are smaller spells, rituals, and acts of Magic done to enchant each step of the way to your goal. They can make all the difference.

In the previous example, the Dzambhala offering rite was the macro-enchantment. It could have been a novena, or a candle spell, or a Mojo Hand, a bath, or anything that is designed to get me a better job than the one I had. The macro-enchantment steers the overall strategy of whatever it is I am trying to do. If I have a well-designed strategy to achieve my desires, it boosts the probability of success, overcomes obstacles, and generally greases the wheels of the universe. If I do not have a clear path to my goal, as was the case here, it creates opportunities and brings needed information.

Macro-enchantments are usually the only spell that people do on a single issue. Sometimes they are enough. Some people believe that doing more than one act of Magic toward a goal is disrespectful or shows lack of faith to whatever powers were originally invoked. Thankfully, this is not a belief that I share, because it is precisely by discarding this nugget as superstition that I started produce better results in my Magic.

Micro-Enchantment

Vodou Priest Louis Martine once told me, "First comes the working, then comes the work"—the idea being that you do a spell, then follow up with the non-Magical acts. He said this because he was stressing the importance of not neglecting mundane measures to people who might otherwise cast their spell than wait at home for the girl to show up or the check to arrive in the mail. I agree with this sentiment, but it got me thinking about taking it a step further. What if, instead of just Magical acts being followed up by mundane ones, we built a flow chart where Magical actions are followed up by mundane actions that are then boosted and followed up on by more Magical ones? These can then open new avenues for more non-Magical efforts and the pattern repeats. This is where the idea for micro-enchantments comes from.

In the example of my finding the job, the rituals to Manjushri for learning the crash-course in VOIP (Voice Over Internet Protocol), and the Kurukulla spell to help ace the interview were micro-enchantments. The opportunity to employ them only came about because the macro-enchantment with Dharmshala opened up the opportunity for them. You can see this in the following chart.

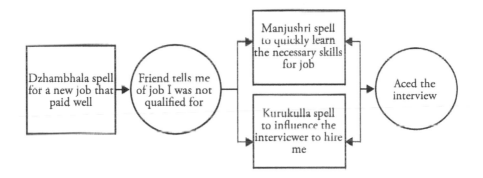

This example is very simple, of course. The chain can get much longer when needed. A client who has been unemployed for a long amount of time recently found an excellent job, but it took a serious amount of work. After a consultation with him, and finding out that he was adept at working with the Greek Gods associated with the planets, we came up with the following chain that eventually landed him a design job that paid twice what his last job did.

In this scheme, you can see that we started with a big Jupiterian macro-enchantment, Jupiter being the planet of expansion and wealth. We also invoked the four virtue Goddesses Abundantia, Gloria, Victoria, and Harmonia to empower a Jupiter Glyph Parchment that he would keep on him until he found a new job.

After this, he went on his social media and contacted friends and former coworkers to let them know he was looking for a job. That Wednesday he did a micro-enchantment short invocation to Mercury and burned an orange candle to ensure that his networking efforts reached the right ears in a speedy way. Shortly thereafter, someone he used to work with told him about a job opportunity and said he should send in his resume. He customized his resume for this job, sent in the digital copy, and printed out a version of it to place on his altar where he would call upon the powers of Helios and chant "Helios Achebukrom" to make it *shine* brighter than all the other resumes that were expected for that position—a number likely in the hundreds. Because the copy on his altar was not one he was sending in, he could dress it with oil and sigils and whatever else he needed. He was scheduled for an interview and took a three-day Crown of Success Bath to make sure that his whole body was immersed in Magic before that interview. He also did a dual invocation to Jupiter and Venus:

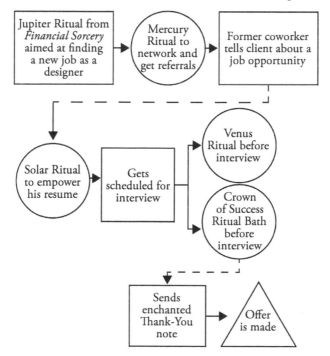

Ay-Eu (the syllables associated with Venus and Jupiter), oh, Aphrodite and Zeus, bearers of beauty and benevolence, bless me before this interview. Aphrodite, bring me charm and beguiling presence. Mighty Zeus, magnetize me with majesty and affluence that I may be hired for this position and glorify your names. So shall it be.

The client landed the job and is living quite happily five years on. He told me that he now uses this combination of macro- and micro-enchantment on projects in his profession and will soon be employing a similar pattern for a promotion he wants to nab.

The Might of Multi-Micro-Magics

One of the great things about using micro-enchantments to follow up on a macro-enchantment is the possibility of approaching the same problem from different angles. This also helps with compensating for problems that can arise when an approach we think is able to be influenced with Magic is not so easily swayed.

A classic example of this would be a court case. You might do a single macro-enchantment to win your case, such as summoning a spirit or performing a court case spell with Psalm 35. This creates an overall blessing on the case and asks the judge to rule in your favor. The micro-enchantments make it more interesting because you can attack the problem from all of the following angles at once:

- ⊛ Once you know who the judge will be, you can gather some personal links, like a picture and signature, to use in a sweetening spell that will help win her over and be as lenient as possible.

- ⊛ Similar links from the opposing attorney (whether it's defense or prosecution) can be used in a confusion spell where their links are held every night over burning poppy-seeds, mullein, and other jinxing herbs.

✪ Your own attorney can be blessed and bolstered with good luck petitions and success spells.

✪ Dirt from the courthouse can be brought to your temple so that you can enchant yourself to win on that ground and to make offerings to the spirits that dwell there.

This approach, where you are pinging all sides with Magic, including the judge and even the place where the case is being heard, is potent because if one of these approaches proved unenchantable, the other approaches still might work. If you were the defendant, and the prosecutor was particularly strident in his work or had some spiritual protection of his own, you might not be able to affect him, yet still charm the judge in your favor. If, however, you could not sway the judge, then perhaps the confusion spell would be enough to get the case thrown out. There are a lot of variables in every situation and using multiple micro-enchantments increases your success rate dramatically.

The Take-Away

This key addresses multiple problems. How do we approach a problem with numerous spell types? How can we deepen the use of Magic in a strategy? How can we ensure success? How do we keep multiple Magics all cohesive? Harold is presenting Salphegor with a long list of enchantments in this key's comic. Thankfully, most powerful demons have staff for this kind of thing; you will find them in the Grimoires as "legions."

The macro/micro mix will allow you to hit your problems from different angles and use a variety of techniques. Your micro-enchantments could involve energetic work, candle spells, and spirit-summoning, all aimed at the same goal. Similarly, we can cover multiple angles, so that if influencing key people turns out to be unenchantable, other spells aimed at creating beneficial chance might have better luck. We keep all these disparate parts of our strategy bound together and overseen by the one macro-enchantment that steers the whole effort.

All this goes a long way in solving the one big problem we are always trying to solve: How do I obtain my goal?

Key 11:
You Are a Spirit Too

For much of the 1980s and '90s, when I was first learning Magic, it was a popular idea in Occult circles to think that spirits, Gods, and other powers were all simply mental constructs of the Magician. Aleister Crowley commented that "The spirits of each Goetia are portions of the Human Brain."[1] Lon DuQuette famously says, "Magic is all in your head; you just have no idea how big your head is."[2] Chaos Magic took this even further and made the spirits completely irrelevant, stating that Scrooge McDuck was just as effective as the Archangel of Jupiter, possibly more so.

Thankfully, with the turning of the millennium came a different attitude toward the spirits. Occultists began returning to the Grimoires and traditions of the past, and Chaos Magicians started to find that, contrary to what they had been told, the spirits *did* matter and that Scrooge McDuck was a poor substitute for Clauneck.

Sadly, humans seem to be really bad at finding middle ground for anything, and so no sooner did spirits once again take their rightful place in the arcana of Magic, did people start arguing that spirits were responsible for *all* Magic. People began to discuss a "spirit model" that was opposed to an "energy model" or "mental model"—as if Magic has to contain itself to just one means of working. The idea that all Magic is performed by outside spirits takes us away from the simple fact that we are spirits.

Spirits in the Material World

Just like the Police song "Spirits in the Material World," trapped within these deteriorating sacks of protoplasm is a luminous and powerful spirit—some would even say a God. In fact, for as hard on humanity as Christianity can be, even Jesus pointed out that "I said, ye are Gods."[3]

Beings we commonly call spirits and Gods do not have bodies and manifest across a spectrum that is hard for us to even fully conceptualize. We *do* possess bodies and are, at least for this lifetime, trapped in this hard-edged world of form, but within that body is a spirit. The body is not necessarily a bad thing, though. Indeed, one of the things that spirits find enjoyable about offerings is the foothold into the material that we have naturally. We are constrained by the body for sure, but that does not mean we have no access to Magic that is facilitated entirely by our own spirit, mind, and—yes—body.

You know how I first knew Magic was real? I wanted something to happen, concentrated on it happening, held my breath, *felt* with my mind for the future that I was aiming for, and kind of mentally *shifted* myself to that reality. No spirits. No angels. No Gods. If that sounds like a vague description of what happened, that's because the explanation takes an entire course to unpack, but the actual doing of it was simple and natural—because I am a spirit, and spirits are capable of doing spirit shit!

I am not alone. Many of the people who have been called Witches or healers through the years do not necessarily have spirit familiars, ceremonial systems, or anything that they study as Magic. They are just people whose inner life was able to spill out into their outer life—because they are spirits.

We are spirits. That's why in Tibetan Magic, you have training to raise the body temperature through breath, to breathe mantras into other people, even to switch bodies if the Yogas of Naropa are to be believed! That is why people that try Sex Magic usually are successful with it. That is why some people can heal with their hands, other can prophesize, and yet others can simply will things to happen. It is why Spare could cast a sigil that would bring the roof caving in, or why William S. Burroughs could curse a place by sitting in front of it, playing the sounds he recorded the day before but in reverse.

Am I saying not to summon spirits or invoke the Gods? No! If you have read this far, you have already read about times that I or my students have worked with spirits to fruitful ends. What I am saying is that you are part of the process of Magic whether you work with spirits or not. Your abilities, actions, and mind all play a role in the outcome.

Spirits Teaching Spirits

One of the fun things that can happen is that spirits evoked by a Magician often end up telling the Sorcerer *how* to do something rather than just doing it themselves. Imagine thinking that all Magic happens because of spirits, and the first thing the spirit does is insist that you do it yourself! They may instruct you on gesture, energy, breath, or materia that will either aid you in your work or enable you to do the Magic yourself entirely. Sometimes these are the very things that get passed on in traditions of Magic, Witchcraft, Tantra, and even mainstream religions. Sometimes the tricks they teach are just for that one operation, never to be repeated.

In the last apartment I rented before buying a house, a neighbor moved in next door who was excessively loud at all hours of the night. Attempts to talk to my neighbor and get him to act like an adult resulted in threats and belligerence. I decided to perform an expulsion ritual, commonly known as a hot footing. I laid down hot-foot powder, prayed the Psalms, and asked hot spirits to make him move. I did everything right, but I got bupkis for my efforts. If anything, the hot energy circulating around seemed to make him louder and more unbearable. So, I conjured a familiar spirit that I work with and asked what needed to be done. She instructed that to make this person move, what I needed to do was stand in the street in front of his house in the middle of the night and listen to the song "Sinnerman" by Nina Simone. That's it. Just stand and stare and listen.

It sounds stupid, right? But that's what I did, and when I did it, I understood. I stood out there angry at him for being such a bad neighbor, and identifying this anger with the driving music seemed to amplify it and sharpen it. As the words came up I ground my teeth and imagined him as the Sinnerman; I pictured him running to the rock looking for a place to take shelter from the Magic. But everyplace he goes to hide, he is shunned. Listen to the song and you will know what I mean.

Just like in the song, he runs bleeding to the river, then to the sea and is rebuffed. He prays to the Lord, but the lord tells him to go to the Devil who was waiting. Then as Nina Simone shouts, "Power!" (*Power*

Lord!), I felt my own power growing and pressing upon him. I was good and truly in a trance. I could feel the powders that I had previously laid down suddenly spring to life. I could see spirits that are attracted to this wrathful working come and infest his dwelling. It was satisfying and draining and powerful—and all I did was stare and listen to a song, allowing to guide me into using my own powers of spirit to do the work I needed done.

And done it was. He started staying away from home more often and eventually broke his lease and left less than a month after my spell. I don't know why; I just know that he skulked out in the middle of the night like a Sinnerman looking for shelter. Good riddance. As soon as he left, I went and cleansed his apartment and did a solid cleansing of all those wrathful energies and entities. I was living next door, after all, and wanted to attract a new, quieter neighbor.

This approach is not something I would have thought to do myself, and it's something that some people who are very hung up on Occult trappings probably think is stupid. The fact is, though, that it worked. A spirit provided the instructions, but it was me, as a spirit, doing the Magic. It gave me new respect for the power of music in Magic, but in the end, I doubt the experiment would be effective if repeated. It was a one-time instruction.

Leaving the Body

Of course, nowhere is it more evident that we are spirits than when we have an out-of-body experience, traveling in the spirit vision, or in lucid dreams. A full discussion of the methods of creating an out-of-body experience is beyond the room we have in this book,[4] but I assume most readers are familiar with the concept.

In the astral body, one can visit others, implant ideas, and perform direct healing, cursing, or blessing on people, just as would a spirit that was summoned. One of the most fruitful things you can do with a spirit you encounter in the astral is ask how to perform acts of Magic that they themselves perform. Just like my local spirit instructed me to listen to a song and stare, you might get something simple, or as with my encounters with Hekate, you might get something so complex it takes more than a decade to learn and master. The spirits can give the most amazing responses about how to hold the mind, raise the voice, and gesticulate the body—all making Magic.

Energy

As spirits once again took their rightful place amongst Magicians in this century, "energy" became the new thing that people frowned upon speaking of. Yet, it's probably the best term in English we have for concepts like *prana* and *chi*, as well as the Elemental Powers and Magnetic Fluid written about by early 20th century Occultists like Franz Bardon, whose *Initiation Into Hermetics* is one of the best Magical training manuals of all time.

In that book, Bardon describes how to infuse a room, an object, or even a person with elemental energy patterned to a specific purpose. In the early 1990s, Matthew Brownlee and I threw a party during which we use used Bardon's techniques to charge different rooms according to the elements. By the end of the party, people in the Air-infused kitchen were having lively intellectual conversations, people in the Earth-infused living room were sitting like lumps watching television, people in my Water-charged bedroom were having heart-to-heart emotional sharing discussions, and people in Matt's Fire-charged room were doing...let's just say passionate things.

This idea of using energy in Magic directed by the Magician is widely used in Tibetan Tantra as *tron-du*, the sending and receiving of lights: hooked red lights that charm people with the power of the mantra you are chanting, golden lights that bring wealth with the power of Dzambhala, white rays that bestow the healing power of Tara when you blow on a patient's wound. All energy able to be directed by us because *we are spirits.*

The Take-Away

Salphegor wants to get Harold to take some responsibility, or at least participate in the Magic he is trying to do. Harold doesn't seem open to it. He doesn't see himself as a spirit. The problem this key addresses is the problem Sorcerers face when they stop being part of the Magic and their practice turns into buying or begging favors from Gods, demons, or whatever you can get to listen.

You matter in the equation and you need to figure out what your role is in the strategy. What role does the verbal, mental, or material actions you take play in your spell? If there are none, what can you add of yourself? How does this working feed or further you as a spirit?

Key 12:
Check Your Links

Did your spell fail?

Did the demon not accomplish its task?

Did the Hoodoo that you do, not know who to do the Hoodoo to?

Sorcerers and web developers share a problem that might be the culprit: bad or missing links, which is our 12th Key of Spellcrafting.

Prayers for intercession are just utterances to a power that you hope will intercede on your behalf. As we have seen, Sorcery is a bit more active than that. We *expect* a result and are participating in the process of getting it done. One of the ways that we participate and make our Sorcery more than simple prayers is by providing a Magical link.

Links to people, places, or even situations are essential to Sorcery, and when I talk to students and clients about spells that that fell short of the mark, the lack of a good link is often the problem.

What Are Links?

Think of the Magical link as a targeting system for Sorcery. It is how your spell, spirit, or power knows who or what to effect. Taking the time to provide a good link will help your Magic from yielding up the proverbial *"404 Not Found."*

We have shown that Sorcery is good at influencing events and minds. The amount of influence it has on any given situation depends on many factors: degree of probability, powers of the forces invoked, the gifts and development of the Sorcerer, and a way to grab hold of the material world. This last thing is what the link provides.

Because Magic works with spiritual, energetic, and unseen forces, the material links bring it into the world of form.

What Makes a Good Link?

Like most things in Magic, it is not a matter of simply having something or not. If this book accomplishes one thing, I hope that it's breaking people out of simplistic binary thinking. Links are not all created equal. They can be rated according to relevancy and intimacy.

As far as intimate links go, the most classic links to a person you want to affect are of course hair and fingernails. Not only are these intimately connected to the person, but they are regularly discarded and easily gotten from a bathroom trashcan, hairbrush, or a Supreme Court Justice's soda can.[1]

Sometimes people go the extra mile and steal unwashed underwear, thinking that if it's something a bloodhound could sniff out to find someone, it might be even better for Magic. This is not unsound thinking; in fact, there are some types of necromancy in which the bones of a dog as well as that of a human are used so that the dog can hunt down a target for the human spirit.

If you are not willing or able to get the nasty bits, a signature is a good link too. Even a digital picture of a signature from a scanned document can be a great link, as it is that person's assertion of selfhood. Like a politician's attack ad, it says "Yes, this is me and I authorize this message."

Pictures are okay, but in practice, they work best alongside of other links. Lots of people look like you, after all. You might argue that the picture, being a captured image of a specific person, is even better than a signature, but there is something about the power of names and sigils that seems to make it better. Pictures can help you focus and visualize, and some people swear by them, but for me the link that you use in a spell should be more direct than that.

Apart from intimacy, relevancy is also important. If you are trying to influence someone's mind, hair from their head is best. If you are trying to cultivate more sex in your marriage, hair from lower on the body would be better. If it's someone at work, then an item that he or she uses on the job would be more relevant than something he or she uses on weekends.

If you are trying to limit someone's movements or get them to leave a place, the dirt from their footprint is a classic link. Think symbolically.

Links to Place

Not all links are to people. Often it links to a place that you need. Dirt is the number-one link. The reason that graveyard dirt works so well as a component of spells is that it is a link to the spirit whose grave the dirt was purchased from. Footprints work because they are a link to the person who made the print. Dirt from other places can be taken or purchased in the same way. The earth holds memory, and the dirt from someone's home can be used to effect the people in that home. The dirt from key places in a town or city can be used to effect events and laws and patterns within that city.

One of my students, who prefers to remain anonymous, put together a list of places to gather dirt from that are outside the graveyard/crossroads box:

- ⊛ From near a legislature building to promote dialogue and working together.
- ⊛ From a newspaper office or post office to aid the spread of an idea.
- ⊛ From a hospital for healing (use due diligence and check out the success rate of that particular hospital for the illness you're dealing with).
- ⊛ From an outdoor art sculpture for artistic talent and ideas.
- ⊛ From a sports arena for athletic ability or for winning a contest that involves skill (again, pick a team that doesn't objectively suck).
- ⊛ From a hotel or airport to increase opportunity for travel.
- ⊛ From a river bank for releasing of ideas/relationships/etc.
- ⊛ From Graceland, if you're trying to get arrested.[2]

There are a lot of other things we can grab from a place other than dirt, of course. Mitt Romney famously referenced the Citizens United SCOTUS decision by saying, "Corporations are people, my friend." Well if corporations are people, then logos are links! So are contracts. So is someone's desk nameplate. If corporations want to be people, treat them like people and bless them for doing well and jinx the crap out of them when they do ill.

Sorcerous Sabotage

If you can't grab links from a target person or dirt from a place, you can always bring your Magic to them. On the positive side of things, this is exactly what a talisman is: a bit of Magic that captures the power of a ritual, a spirit, or an astrologically potent moment and brings that influence to the wearer. The talisman is a link.

On the less savory side of Sorcery, this is where planting hot-foot power and goofer dust somewhere that your target will walk comes into play, but you shouldn't limit yourself to powders. Planting sigils behind pictures, condition oils in shampoos, and Trojan gifts are all tricks I have seen done. Sorath, the Demon of the Sun, once instructed me to plant a mirror with his sigil on it so that the reflection would shine into a certain office room every day. That was a jinx, but I used the same tactic with a different spirit to promote healing as well. It was an effective technique that I have employed a few times now.

In Political Magic, the two biggest problems are that famous people have thousands of people directing prayers and spells their way for their protection and undoing. This makes your spell just one influence among thousands. The other problem is that it is hard to get a direct link and certainly not worth the legal trouble one might get into. One wonders what Martin Shkreli wanted with Hillary Clinton's hair? Whatever it was, I am sure it wasn't worth going to jail for.

Planting Magical links at the site that someone will be speaking gets around both of these issues. Your spell has more impact because the target is standing where the link is directly, and you don't need any link to bring back to your temple.

Is It Good Enough?

Just because you have a good link, doesn't mean it's good *enough*. People get too binary and caught up in thinking something either works or it doesn't, when they should be thinking about things on a scale from good to better to best. Even if you have a link, that doesn't mean your spell wouldn't perform better with an improved one.

Many years ago, a friend asked me to jinx and confuse someone who was doing something bad I can't mention. I don't do stuff like that for hire, so please don't ask, but for a friend and a good cause—sure. He gave me a digital photo of the person, his name, his birthdate, and such. That is usually enough, but as I did the work at home, I could *feel it* just going nowhere. It was like trying to spray someone with a water hose when they are behind a glass door.

My friend was telling me that the confusion was having some effect, but when I questioned him further, I felt like it was meager and would fall short of what we needed to prevent this person from doing the terrible thing we were trying to stop.

So I took the Magic to the man instead of the man to the Magic. I got an address for the target and went to lay confusion powder on his door-step, but as I approached, floodlights turned on. Not wanting to get in trouble for stepping on this guy's lawn at 3 a.m., I went home. The next day, I purchased a Super Soaker water gun and painted it up with appropriate sigils. I dissolved the powder in some war water and re-consecrated it. That night at 3 a.m., I used the Super Soaker to "dress" the target's front porch without ever setting foot on the property.

Suddenly all the Magic I had been doing had a clear route and the floodgates opened. *Mischief managed.*

Living In a Material World

Sometimes it's not about linking to a person or place, so much as it is just giving an operation something material to grab on to. Folk Magic is often inherently material, but all the high Magic, spirit-evoking, demon-compelling stuff took on new effectiveness when I realized that offerings formed a material link to help give material result.

The same is true of Sympathetic Magic performed with the aid of an invoked or even fully conjured spirit. If you have a spirit in front of you and make a packet that binds a link to the spirits seal, you will have a potent way for that spirit to know what to do, as well as a path for its influence to travel over. This method gets used a lot in the Caribbean and West Africa, where the DeLaurence printings of Grimoires were so valued in spell work that DeLaurence himself was seen as a white-suited Sorcerer, and the company catalogue considered a black book all on its own.[3]

Those who eschew material parts of Magic in favor of the psychic/psionic/energetic work, as well as New Thought practitioners who "will" things to happen, might find their efforts bolstered by having a good link to hold and focus on when performing their exercise. For one student of mine, this lesson on links seems to be the *only* lesson she has implemented, but claims it has increased her effectiveness many times over. She is now an avid collector of personal links to just about everyone she meets, as well as a compiler of dirt from key places in her life. She has these all catalogued and labeled in a large chest so that they are ready for use.

Whatever you are trying to achieve, I find that very often the missing link is, well, a link!

The Take-Away

Harold is presenting Salphegor with links to his target. He maybe went a little overboard with it, but it's better than a picture printed from someone's Facebook profile. How does *your* Magic get from you to the target? That is the problem that we are seeking to solve in this key.

What links can you incorporate into your working? Are those links sufficient or are there better links? How relevant and intimate are the links you have? Asking yourself these questions is the key to thinking like a Sorcerer and solving this age-old problem.

Key 13:
Practice Sane Eclecticism

We live in a world where the secrets of Magic and esoteric religion are mostly cracked wide open for all the world to see. It is natural, therefore, for people to engage more than one tradition in their work. We also live in a world that is more fully aware of privilege and the problems of cultural appropriation. Some would say we are *too* aware and have perhaps overreacted by doing things like shutting down college yoga classes and protesting corporate mindfulness programs because they appropriate Eastern culture.

I am not here to tell you what to think about social issues, but these are not the only concerns when it comes to eclecticism and mixing traditions. There are issues of effectiveness as well as safety when you are mixing thing up. Just like people, some Gods and spirits are open to new or loose approaches, and others are quite conservative. Because of my own eclectic background and training, this balance between eclecticism and tradition is something that I think about often.

One the one hand, the great gift of our age is that the doors have all been more or less thrown open. We have unprecedented access to Magical and religious practices that people in previous decades never dreamed possible. This is not *only* because of the internet either. I grew up in a small town in rural central New Jersey, and before I was 20 years old, I had learned Magic from a Wiccan Priestess, an African-American Conjure Man, a Santera, a Rosicrucian/Ceremonial Magician, and most importantly a Buddhist Lama. Lama Vajranatha (John Myrdhin Reynolds) is the first Westerner to receive Ngakpa robes (Ngakpas are non-celibate Sorcerer Priests). Not only did he become my revered teacher, but he introduced me to the OTO and Witchcraft scenes in New York, which he was a part of in the 1970s.

If I was to just pick only one tradition, or restrict myself only to those cultures that I was ethnically connected to, I feel like it would be a betrayal of what the universe presented me with: a beautiful array of traditions and people willing to share them.

On the other hand, we have people that are so loose and eclectic that it is, to be frank, silly. This is the Wiccan who tells you Kali is her Goddess and Jesus is her God—meanwhile she knows almost nothing about either one. This is the person who announces that they practice Phurba—but what they mean is that they use it as an Athame to cast circles and have never studied with a teacher or even read anything about Tibetan Buddhism. This is the ceremonialist replacing the Archangels with the Orishas in the LBRP because he read a book and wants to play Lukumi Priest. This is Aleister Crowley when he tried to tackle Taoism, which he clearly knew nothing about. And yes, this has been me too, stumbling around drawing a veve of Legba in the snow.... The fact that it seemed to work does not make it authentic Vodou; it merely points out that the Gods sometimes favor drunkards and fools.

So how do we walk the line? How do we take advantage of the access that, I believe, is the great gift of the age, without falling into dilettantism, delusion, or danger?

The question is different for different people, but I have some rules that I follow in my work. Following these guidelines has allowed me to put together my own Magical system and style that draws upon traditions new and old, yet still allow me to be taken seriously by most traditionalists.

Do Not Usurp Titles

This is by far the most important rule. If you read a book on Vodou, it does not make you a Houngan or Mambo. If you read every book on it ever written, memorize 12 CDs worth of songs, and spend every weekend drawing veves and invoking the Loa, it *still* does not make you a Houngan or Mambo, because that is based on an initiation. You can be a Vodousant, and you may even know more than many initiated Houngans out there (more on that in a minute), but you still have not been initiated, so don't take the title.

This is not just about personal titles. You should not usurp the titles of traditions or tools either. You can read books on Dzogchen. You can do the practices. You can even attain the result. But if you have not had the introduction to mind from a Guru, you are not doing Dzogchen.

The same practice, no longer in context, is something else, so call it something else.

No one can tell you what to do, and don't let anyone tell you who to pray to. We have religious and Magical freedom after all, and a good deal of the history of Magic has been made by people who step beyond what is allowed and make the orthodoxy upset. So you can make a spirit pot. You can even study and draw upon how Ngangas are constructed, but unless you do it in that tradition, it is not that thing and should not be called that. Words have meaning and you cheapen and corrupt the reputation of practice when you pretend at it.

Even If You Hold a Title, Don't Throw It Around Until You Know Something Real

This is the flip-side of the previous rule and is something that not a lot of people talk about, including traditionalists. It is possible currently to get the coveted initiations, but still know next to nothing. Houngan Hector here in New Jersey told me that shortly after he developed an interest in Vodou, he flew down to Haiti and was initiated Houngan Asogwe along with a bunch of other people who were very new to Vodou. This is the highest level of initiation. He flew down, did his thing, and flew back. The problem was that he only knew a handful of songs and some other things that he gleamed from books. Now, much to Hector's credit, he flew back down again and again, and found people to give him the training that he knew he wanted. Other people, however, are happy with the title and just use it to validate whatever they make up.

The same thing happens in the East. You can be born a Tulku (recognized incarnation) and be enthroned as a Lama without ever going on retreat. One famous Lama was the subject of a paternity suit that he eventually lost. Some true believers thought that he must be innocent because Tantra teaches how to hold back your semen during orgasm, and therefore he wouldn't get someone pregnant by accident. The problem with this line of thinking is that this Rinpoche probably did not ever master that technique or many others you might expect. He was a Tulku by birth and spent most of his life in the West. He can write books on pop psychology and anything else he wants, and it will be passed off as the words of a master as long as his name is attached. Often you find situations where the translator and scholar knows more than the priest or initiate who has been fortunate enough, or rich enough, to buy themselves a title and a silly hat.

I can fall into the same trap if I'm not careful. I am a Bishop because I have been consecrated as such, but I don't throw the term around much because I have not had (nor am I desiring) the training that I would get in a mainstream seminary. I am what is called an Episcopi Vagantes, or "Wandering Bishop." I transmit the sacraments when asked and I have Magical pursuits where this is important, but I don't try to use that title to add validity to teachings that are otherwise not related to that work. Hopefully you are reading this book because I have 30 years of experience with spells, not because I have special initiations or holy orders.

Separate Symbol Sets from Tech

Systems of Magic can be broken down into symbol sets and tech. Symbol sets are usually dependent on culture, time, tradition, and sometimes only available through initiation. They are the Gods, spirits, and symbols of a path. Using a symbol set outside of its culture or initiatory stream can sometimes be difficult, disrespectful, or even downright dangerous. Tech, on the other hand, works because it works, and thus can be looked at and examined from outside of any specific tradition. In this way, you can find the most effective techniques without falling into the trap of making an eclectic mess. For example, it would be fine to borrow the idea of multiplying offerings with the mind from Tibetan Buddhism and use it in Wicca. It would be quite another to grab the nearest Phurba and call it your Athame, using it in the way that an Athame is used without really learning anything about the Tibetan Phurba traditions.

Iron being apotropaic, triangles trapping or manifesting spirits, circles as protection and microcosms, lucid arising in dreams—these things work because they work. There is tech there that is beyond anyone's claim of propriety. Focusing on these aspects of a path or tradition, you will be able to glean usable things from studying other traditions without being disrespectful.

Context Matters

Recent university studies of Tummo, Tibetan Yoga of Inner Heat, have confirmed that you can control core body temperature with breath and mind.[1] You can even do it outside of the context of Tantric training. There are physical and mental health benefits. This is a good thing to do whether you are a Tantrika or not. It is a good thing to do whether you are a Buddhist or not. However, if you are not doing it within that context, it is no longer Tummo at that point.

I think it is great and cool to learn how to do Tummo and gain the health benefits, but outside of Tantra, it is no longer Tummo. It is something else. When I teach it outside of Tantra, I tend to use the phrase "inner heat." It is a useful and potent method of producing power and mystical bliss. But I avoid the term "Tummo" because that has a specific context.

You can do as you like, no one can tell you who to pray to, but if you take something from one tradition and use it in another, expect that it will change. Context is everything.

Approach Any Tradition from Its Own Base

The Chakras are not the Sephira. If you try and approach the Chakras as Sephira, you will not understand them at all. You will probably mess up your understanding of Sephira, as well, in the process. Freya is not just another Venusian Archetype. She is different.

Recently someone in one of my classes was asked if they do the Middle Pillar ritual. They replied that they do not, but that they do my Pillar and Spheres exercise from *The Sorcerer's Secrets* instead. Although I am honored by anyone doing my rituals, the two rituals are completely different and have almost nothing in common with one another. Yes, they both activate points on the body, but Pillars and Spheres sets up an alchemical reaction among the five elements by placing them in a certain order. The Middle pillar is an attempt to map and activate the Tree of Life onto the body and is not the same thing. Similarly, most systems of yoga that work with the seven chakras most are familiar with are different from either of these. Often I find people are way too interested in trying to mix everything together in one bland stew than to realize that differences are important and often what makes a thing truly useful.

When you approach a different system, try as much as possible to forget what you know about other systems for at least a while. Approach it as a complete newbie so you can view it on its own terms and from its own base.

Decide on the Level of Involvement You Want and Don't Confuse It

An argument that people have used against practicing more than one Magical system, and even against raising children in more than one religion, is that any given path takes a lifetime to master. This is true. I could spend the rest of my life living in Nepal and studying Himalayan Magic and never learn it all. You can spend your entire life as a Kimbanda Priest and never exhaust what there is to learn and master. You can be Catholic from birth until death and never completely master the whole thing. You can spend 30 hours a week practicing Tai Chi and still never get as good as Chen Xiouwang. All this is true.

But remember in the last key when I talked about competence, mastery, and perfection? Sometimes you don't want to master something. You just want to gain competency, and that takes a lot less time. You can spend your life studying German and learning to master the language, but for most of us, the ability to hold conversations is enough, and it doesn't take that long to learn that. Being a martial arts master is wonderful and amazing, but for most people, learning enough to maintain health, defend themselves in a fight, and maybe have some fun sparring will not be a lifetime obsession. I am a nut about meditation and would spend hours in meditation a day if I could. A guy who works at the insurance company, however, might only want to lower his stress levels, gain some control over his thoughts, and be happier, in which case, 20 minutes a day will do him a world of good.

People who are competent in multiple areas become masters of making connections that specialists lose the ability to see. Look at the CEOs of the world. Do you think Steve Jobs was the best design person at Apple? Was he the best accountant? Was he the best technician? The best marketer? Probably not. He could, however, see connections that maybe others could not and bring these all together in ways that others could not.

Competency is fine—great, in fact. I like it. I forget who said it, but specialization is for insects. Just don't confuse competency with mastery.

The Take-Away

In our comic, Harold is trying to call Jesus through a Tibetan Phurba that he has consecrated to Odin. I wish that this was some comic nonsense that Matt and I made up, but it's not. People have done that and worse. Don't be Harold.

This key attempts to address two problems: The first is tendency for people to become too wildly eclectic and combine cultures and traditions in ways that are unhelpful, to put it mildly. The second is for people who veer to the other edge of orthodoxy and separation, feeling that no two cultures or traditions should ever be mixed—as if that was ever historically a reality.

It's actually pretty simple. If you encounter a tradition you are interested in, make the effort to learn and respect it. Don't take titles that you don't have. Don't downplay influences to justify your involvement. Just because European Grimoires have played a small part in Hoodoo does not mean that Hoodoo is not African-American at its core. You can still practice it if you aren't, but you need to respect where it comes from and not pass off your own innovations as tradition. You also should realize that some things are made for initiates only, and you run a real risk when mimicking those practices without a pass, or worse, reading a single book and throwing together a ritual with powers you do not remotely understand.

If you do that, and people still have a problem with you, take advice from Robert Downey, Jr.: "Listen, smile, agree, and then do whatever the fuck you were gonna do anyway."[2]

Key 14:
Magic Is a Rhizome

Magic is not neat and tidy. It is not linear and predictable. I have written the keys in this book in order for you to be able to use Magic skillfully to achieve both your material and spiritual goals, but that doesn't mean that things will happen in the ways you expect. Magic is a *Rhizome*.

Now unless you are a botanist or a philosopher, you might not know what a Rhizome is. A Rhizome is a subterranean network of stems that sends roots and shoots from all nodes. They are unpredictable and defy linear and hierarchal organization in the way that say, a tree would conform to. Different philosophers have used the Rhizome as a metaphor for the spread of information, media, culture, and even consciousness.

Psychologist and mystic Carl Jung pointed out:

Life has always seemed to me like a plant that lives on its rhizome. Its true life is invisible, hidden in the rhizome. The part that appears above ground lasts only a single summer. Then it withers away—an ephemeral apparition. When we think of the unending growth and decay of life and civilizations, we cannot escape the impression of absolute nullity. Yet I have never lost a sense of something that lives and endures underneath the eternal flux. What we see is the blossom, which passes. The rhizome remains.[1]

Magic is like this, a force that rests under the surface, blooming above the surface when Magicians wield it. This is true of individual spells, entire traditions, and indeed the whole of Magic itself. Of course, one of the problems of the Rhizome is its refusal to be contained and conform to a structure. The Rhizomal nature of Magic is one reason that Magic has been so feared, and why those who wield it are vilified by people who like a nice, orderly universe.

Spell Spread

Speaking about the Rhizomic spread of culture in his book *1000 Plateaus*, Gilles Deleuze noted something that I feel applies to Magic as well: "Rhizome has no beginning or end; it is always in the middle, between things, interbeing, intermezzo."[2] The journal *Rhizomes: Cultural Studies in Emerging Knowledge* notes further:

> ...spreads like the surface of a body of water, spreading towards available spaces or trickling downwards towards new spaces through fissures and gaps, eroding what is in its way. The surface can be interrupted and moved, but these disturbances leave no trace, as the water is charged with pressure and potential to always seek its equilibrium, and thereby establish smooth space.[3]

The philosophy of how this applies to Magical traditions and Magic overall is worth pondering, but it is this *spread* applied to specific spells that I want to address in this key. Spells spread into all areas of our lives and even the lives of those around us. That's how they work. Some have suggested that spell results are like water, and take the path of least resistance to their goal, but in practice, they are more Rhizomic and resist even that organizational restriction. I have often looked back and wondered why my Sorcery seemed to take the most winding and perplexing route to manifest and affected so many other things along the way.

Knowing that your Magic will spread in unanticipated ways is important. We can use caveats as discussed in Key 6 to limit the ways our spells can damage people, always remembering that the more we limit things the more we restrict our outcomes, but that doesn't mean that we will be able to control exactly how our Magic manifests and what it influences. Likewise, we can do whatever we can to make our life more enchantable, as per the instructions in Key 3, but that doesn't mean we will be able to have a full grasp on it.

After my second book came out, and I decided to make a go of being a Teacher of Sorcery as a serious career. I was putting a lot of hours in at night, but still needed to keep my full-time day job to pay the bills and put food on the table. I did a spell to increase my customers and income from Strategic Sorcery and immediately lost my day job right afterward. That's the Rhizome for you; the spell spread. It seemed to me like the path of least resistance would have been to simply bring more people into my course. Instead, it removed a desperately needed day job, which did in the end give me more time to work on Strategic Sorcery, gaining more customers and income.

This is where Divination comes in handy, telling us not only whether our work will succeed or not, but also whether its manifestation will have any unforeseen effects as it spreads into areas of our life that we did not intend. It is important to keep in mind Donald Rumsfeld's famous assessment that in any situation "there are known knowns; there are things we know we know. We also know there are known unknowns; that is to say we know there are some things we do not know. But there are also unknown unknowns—the ones we don't know we don't know."[4]

Divination can help with these unknown unknowns, but even the best diviner is not fool-proof. They see what they see. Anyone that claims otherwise can prove me wrong by providing a solid projection of which five companies in the S&P 500 will have the biggest gains next year. You can be right, and we can get rich at the same time. The Rhizome of Magic refuses even to conform to divination.

Avoid Conflicting Spreads

Another problem that the Rhizomic nature of Magic presents is that it can be very hard to manage conflicting spreads at the same time.

A few years back, I was doing some work for a dear friend going through a divorce. I won't get into too many specifics, but it involved work designed to push people away and get them out of your life. It was working out very well. During this same period, I was also doing work to draw clients to a local business, but that work was not panning out very well. When I did a divination and investigation to determine why, the spirits I was consulting informed me that it is very hard for spirits and energies of increase and attraction to take hold while I am simultaneously dealing with spirits of decrease and repulsion. Each of these spells was spreading through my life but the spells for increasing were being choked out by the repelling Sorcery that I had begun first.

Another way to look at this would be like surrounding yourself with people of a certain type. Doing spells like hot-footing, binding, and so on, surround you with spirits and energies that might be akin to surrounding yourself with tough enforcers, gang members, or otherwise violent people. Doing spells to build a business and bring in extra income would be a very different crowd of spirits or people. Suffice to say, it is hard to hold a party where both a gang of soccer hooligans *and* the Rotary Club are both invited. These are difficult Rhizomes to have growing in your life at the same time.

Spell Bleed

Spells you do, even for others, tend to bleed into your life. Therefore after casting a curse, many Rootworkers take a hyssop bath and recite Psalm 51 ("Purge me with hyssop, and I shall be clean: wash me, and I shall be whiter than snow") to stop the bleed of that spell into their life. Exorcists recite the same Psalm before performing an exorcism to clear themselves of the Rhizomic nature of what they perceive as sin, and which might hamper their abilities to perform the exorcism.

This is why many people who have altars to "hot" spirits, beings that are not necessarily evil but are perhaps overly passionate and wrathful, keep those altars outside the house. Of course, because we ourselves are spirits, we are never fully separated from the work we do, and people who routinely engage in wrathful solutions to problems find themselves surrounded by such energies and spirits at all times. Jim Rohn once suggested that we are all the average of the five people we spend the most time with. I don't believe it's quite that simple, but just like our personalities are effected by the people we surround ourselves with, they are effected by the spirits and powers we traffic in as well.

This is why I recommend that unless you are in a job where violence and restriction are the norm, you limit the amount of time you spend on curses, bindings, jinxes, and such. That stuff bleeds into the rest of your life and messes with the more constructive forces that most of us want to focus on.

Of course, spell bleed is not all bad. Many times, I have done prosperity work for others and received increased prosperity myself. I have often performed healings and felt invigorated and energetic afterward. All of which is, of course, welcome. The Rhizome is not bad; it just is.

Meta Magic Mediators

Sometimes a Sorcerer must do what a Sorcerer must do regardless of how it spreads. If we work on behalf of clients, we may often find ourselves in situations where we have to do exactly what I warn against above and work conflicting Magics, increasing or healing for one client, while pushing away and binding for another. This is what is sometimes referred to as "working with both hands." Usually this term is just thrown around as a label for anyone who will work both malevolent and benevolent Magic, or perhaps with angels and demons as well. There is a sort of neutral moral statement here implying neither good nor evil, but if we view it from the standpoint of the actual mechanics of spells that have competing spreads, both of which bleed into your life, it becomes more complicated than that.

Given the Rhizomic nature of Sorcery, the way it spreads horizontally through the world, finding new spaces to surface and bloom, the way it defies ordinary modes of organization, it can be helpful to have the aid of a power that specializes mediating manifestation and managing Magic itself. This falls under what I like to call Meta-Magic, Magic that effects Magic. Those in ceremonial Magic circles will be familiar with the Holy Guardian Angel spoken of in *The Sacred Magic of Abramelin* as well as the Paredros in the *Papyrii Grecae Magicae*. Both spirits can serve this role if you have done the work to gain their knowledge and conversation, which is no easy task. Many books have been written about just this work. If you can manage it, they become trusted guides and advisors as well as assistants in managing your Magic.

Another thing you can do is to work with a spirit of Magic itself. Just like a God of wealth or love, there are Gods who oversee Magic and Witchcraft. Hekate is who I rely upon in these matters, and she has taught me much during the last 17 years to aid me in managing the Magic I put out into the world. She is the patron of my first book for a reason, and has had an impact on everything I have done.

The Saints and spirits of great practitioners who were once alive is yet another avenue to seek this Magical mediation through. For this, I rely on St. Cyprian, who excels at managing and mediating between powers that might otherwise never mix. In fact, here in the New World, this is one of his major roles, which can be seen in the practices of the Peruvian Curandero's Mesa, or field of power. The mesa is usually laid out on the ground in a very intricate display of power objects divided into two or more fields. In his book *Eduardo El Curandero: The Words of a Peruvian Healer*, Eduardo Calderon Palomino details the three fields of his Mesa: Campo Justiciero, "the field of the divine judge," on the right; the Campo Ganadero, "the field of Satan or the Sly-Dealer" (here Ganadero or Rancher is an epitaph of Satan), on the left; and the Campo Medio, the mediating field of San Cyprian, in the middle. During healings and San Pedro Ceremonies, it is the middle field that is the focus—not a matter of exorcising devils, but of finding a balance between two opposing forces, two competing Rhizomic spell spreads.

Ruperto Navarro, a Peruvian Brujo operating in Trujillo, is another Curandero who made a pact with the Devil as a young man. Because of this pact, he is forbidden from working with Christ or any of the Christian Saints that most Curanderos work with—except for St. Cyprian. Navarro's Mesa is divided into three sections in a similar fashion to other mesas with the notable exception that the Ganadero side for harming is on the right and the Curandero side for healing is on the left—the reverse of traditional associations. St. Cyprian manages the middle field where he not only mediates the left and right sides of the mesa, but acts as the ambassador between Navarro's Diabolism and the Christian world that other Curanderos and most of Navarro's clients operate in.

The Take-Away

The problem that this key seeks to solve are those presented by the unruly and at times unmanageable manifestations of Magic. This is why in our cartoon, Harold is so angry. He has been cursing people and it has bled into his life. Are you considering the ways in which your spells might bleed into your life?

You solve this by managing your spells so that there are not competing spreads working against each other. Purify and cleanse yourself when finished with work whose Rhizomal spread you do not wish to carry. You can also seek the assistance of a mediating spirit whose authority helps manage the powers of Magic itself.

PART 3:
ADVANCING YOUR CRAFT

MOVING BEYOND THE BASICS

Key 15:
Judge Success Skillfully

I have heard more nonsense about how to judge the success of Magic than you might imagine. I have talked a lot of nonsense myself earlier in my career, when I was desperate for success and to show that Magic worked. For something that so many people love and care about, there are very few standards applied to how we judge success, yet success is all I ever hear about. Few people ever admit to Magic not working because that would bring up the possibility that the rest of the world is right and that Magic is not real. This key is not about judging whether Magic is real or not; if you have made it this far, I hope that issue is settled for you. This key is about how to evaluate the Magic you are doing.

Let the first lesson of this key be this: **If you never fail to get a result from the spell, if you never fail at contacting the spirit, if the spirit never says things you don't want to hear, you are not really doing anything at all.**

You are accepting such a low standard of success that either the smallest sign is sufficient for you to be happy, or you are giving in to fantasy. This might be okay for the community at large, but not for yourself or even those close to you. In the Occult social media, we all more or less accept each other's reports at face value. It's a game of "I believe in your superpowers if you believe in mine." This helps keep the peace and allows for communication and validation without being impolite. A higher standard, though, should be applied to yourself as well as to your inner circle of peers and students if you have them. We learn as much or more from owning up to and examining failure as we do from success. This is how we get better at the art, and what this 15th Key of Spellcraft is all about.

The Feelies

Several years ago, I was involved in a working to protect a piece of land from development. This threatened place was one that we considered sacred and powerful, so a group was gathered to perform a ritual to empower the local spirits, bind the developers, and further open the veil of this space to us as Sorcerers. The group gathered in the woods at night, and it was one of those classically witchy moments when the spirits seemed to move between the shadows of the trees in the darkness and you could "see" the power being raised as color against the blackness of night. Everyone was wearing dark robes (I hate wearing robes, but I didn't organize the ritual) and as we chanted and moved in unison, the power that we raised was palpable. During the rite, candle flames jumped in a manner that can only be described as paranormal. After the ritual, everyone spoke about the weird visions we had, and how we could feel the power coursing through us. Our bones left lighter and our skin felt like it would jump right off our bodies. We all agreed that the ritual was a rousing success and one of the most powerful that we had done.

Four weeks later, development began exactly as planned and that area is now an "Active Adult Retirement Community." We did not so much as delay the project by even one hour.

Let's contrast this experience with another ritual a few years after that. This ritual was done with a group of just three people, and its aim was to open better financial opportunities and provide a kind of "life reboot" for the couple I was working with. We did the rite, but there was no paranormal sign during the ritual. The spirits did not speak. There was nothing to see. No one felt any different after the ritual than we did before it. The ritual was carried out and the offerings made in a perfunctory manner with little fanfare. I got the distinct impression that the couple I was working with were so mired in their current troubles that they did not hold out much hope for success. It was uninspiring at best.

Not even five days after that ritual, a high school friend offered a job to one of them. The job would pay for them to move and was in a city with more opportunity than their current town. They got the reboot they were so desperately seeking.

The take-away is obvious: Getting the feelies is not really a sign of success. It is great if a ritual is beautiful and inspiring. It is good if you have an energetic or psychic experience from the ritual. It is even more awesome when there is some incredible synchronicity or paranormal event that occurs within the ritual. But in terms of actual success of a spell objective, none of that means much. This is not to say that the feelies and paranormal shenanigans do not occur with successful rituals. They do. Often. But in and of themselves, they are not a sign of success unless they were the purpose of the spell.

Sometimes the reason that the lightbulbs are exploding, the voices are whispering from between the angles of space, and you sense so much power coursing through you that you feel like Goku from *Dragon Ball Z*, is precisely because it's *not* going to its destination and accomplishing the goals of the spell. All that Magic is hanging around the ritual space and not getting where it needs to go—thus the wonderful feelies and paranormal events.

Maybe it's an insufficient link that's the issue. Perhaps the problem is that it's an unenchantable situation where the odds are just stacked against you too much. Possibly there is counter-Magic being employed against you. Or maybe, the Sorcery just wasn't good enough period. Whatever the reason, the spirits you called and the energy you raised are whipping around the temple messing with people's heads not because of your immense power, but because they don't have anywhere to go. If I had to bet on a reason, I would put my money on a bad link. Go back and read Key 12.

Go Beyond the Binary

Let's say that we got a result that fits the statement of intent enough that we can call it a win. Congratulations, your spell worked! Proof is in the pudding, right? You are now unassailable and your methods should not be questioned. Nope. There is more to evaluating success than just the binary "Did it work? Yes/No." There are other questions to be asked.

Did it work in a short time frame? Did it work according to the wording but not the intent? Did the result come with unexpected complications? Did the spell produce a quality result or could it have been better?

Back in 2009, a friend asked me to make him a spirit bottle for employment. I did and I put a lot into it. Because this person is someone I knew personally I *really* wanted a good result. Unfortunately, despite the effort, it was the middle of the Great Recession, and he was in a professional field crowded with applicants. It was 2010 before he finally got a job. He wrote to tell me that my spell finally worked. I replied that I was happy that he found a job, but eight months is not within the acceptable parameters for me to consider it a success. Rather than just take the win, I worked with him to unpack what happened and brainstorm what I could do to expedite success under these less-than-ideal circumstances.

The next person who needed my help during the recession received a spell that called upon mercurial spirits that would speed things along and help with the networking. I also incorporated dirt from key places in the city where the client was looking for work. It worked much better for the next client.

Speaking of job-finding work, another funny story is when Manman Brigitte, the Haitian Queen of the Boneyard, got me a job interview. Quite a few years back, I had decided that I wanted to get a job with the state so that I would have solid benefits and good job security. I was taking civil service exams, but not getting much luck as far as interviews. It just so happened that I was at a ceremony where Manman Brigitte, Wife of the Baron Samedi and the Loa of Justice and the Grave, was being honored and I was asked to drink for her, to consume the rum in her place. Later that night, in the haze between sleep and awake, she came to me and asked me what I needed from her. I replied that I was just honoring her and did not want anything, but she insisted, so I told her about my troubles finding a job with the state.

One week later, I was called in for an interview for a state job. I would be working four 10-hour days with 3 days off a week, which was my ideal. Best yet, they wanted me to start immediately! That's a huge success, right? Not so fast.... The job was as a security guard at a hospital for the criminally insane—something I was not interested in at all. I could almost hear Manman's Laughter in the air. I got what I asked for— and very much in line with that spirit's nature—but not what I intended at all. I said thanks, but no thanks. It was a success technically, but I could do better.

Spirit Contact

Speaking of spirits, let's talk about what that actually means. I have probably referred to communications with spirits at least a dozen times in this book already, but never got very specific about what the means. It means different things at different times, in fact. Sometimes spirits are evoked and communicate as directly and as clearly as if they were a person in the room. At other times, I enter into a trance and receive either messages that may seem fuzzy because of the nature of trance states, or may be in coded "Twisted Language" that needs to be unpacked symbolically. Still other times, spirits may speak through simplistic methods like divination, flashes of inspiration, and omens, to downright world-shaking mystical visions, where one's entire conception of reality falls away.

These things are certainly not the same and should not be treated as the same. If you are visualizing the Archangel Gabriel in the Western Quarter while performing the Lesser Banishing Ritual of the Pentagram, he does not need to speak or communicate at all; the mere empowering of your visualization with his presence is enough to call it a success. If you are praying to Gabriel during a spell to affect the timing of a project, then a flash of a vision or an indication via divination that he will do the work is a success. If you are doing Trithemius's evocation of Gabriel as Archangel of the Lunar Powers into a crystal held in an ebony Monstrance, then it is his visual appearance and clear communication that you should count as success. Anything less would not be worth the trouble. Yet, I have often had people perform full evocations and tell me that it was a success because they felt the spirit's presence or had a dream afterward. This has happened to me on numerous occasions, but when it does, I don't count it as a success. If I do, it is partial at best.

If you are performing a month's long retreat on Gabriel in order to gain the ability to have prophetic visions in the way that Daniel did, then even a vision of Gabriel in a crystal is insufficient, as what you are seeking is to behold the divinity in its totality in the way that Zachariah, Mary, Mohammad, and Joseph Smith[1] claimed to have beheld him.

We must always ask what level of contact is appropriate for the operation we are performing and the needs that we have. You really don't need to rip the roof off reality in a full evocation to visible appearance just to ask Haniel to help you find a boyfriend; her blessing on a Venus talisman will do the job. On the other hand, let's not pretend that everything is a success when it's not.

Improve Your Perception/Projection Ratio

Even more important than the level of manifestation is the matter of separating your own voice from that of a spirit. I call this the perception/projection ratio. In every communication, we can assume that there is some amount of true perception, and some amount of projection from the person having the communication. Assume that whatever your experience of a spirit is, it is *never* 100 percent pure perception. If even memories and perceptions of physical events are not 100 percent accurate, how much more, then, are communications with subtle forces and non-physical beings subject to our own projections? Work to improve this ratio, but assume that there is always something of the spirit and something of yourself in the communication.

Does the spirit or deity tell you any new information that you didn't already know? Does the spirit or deity ever tell you that you are wrong or disagree with you? Does the spirit or deity ever challenge you?

If the answer to these questions and other questions like them is no, then chances are your projection/perception ratio is skewed too far in the projection side.

You may be bristling as you read this. People *do not like* hearing that treasured communications they have had may be less than completely true. In some of my courses, I routinely dismiss people's visions and communications during the first few months, no matter what they are. For some students, this is the first time that they have ever had someone challenge them on something like this. They have either worked solitary or been part of the Occult social media scene where everything gets validated as a matter of course. It's not that I don't think that what they are experiencing has value or a grain of truth, but I start off rejecting those communications because I want them to strive for deeper communication rather than settling for the surface-level chatter. There is so much more to be had.

So how do we improve this? Meditation is my first and best bit of advice. Even if you never get past the stage of focusing on breath and quickly getting distracted, you are still learning to know your mind. You are learning the feel and sound of your own thoughts, and how to tell when you are distracted from what you are supposed to be focused on. These are important skills to possess and meditation is the best and fastest way to obtain them.

The Take-Away

Harold wants to know how to judge Salphegor's work. Our demon here assures him he will find his rubber ducky, and that then is the proof. Anything less is failure and there should be no quibbling about that. Better to admit a failure than to fake success.

There are still other questions to be asked, though. What can you do to make spells work better, faster, stronger? What different angles can you approach the same problem through?

What level of spirit manifestation do you require? Did Harold need to evoke Sal to perform this task? Probably not. Are you overdoing it by summoning a spirit in full for a simple spell? Are you underperforming by accepting a dream or sign from a complex evocation ritual?

Are you stuck in a binary yes/no for success or embracing a spectrum of results that can be tweaked and improved? If so, re-think it.

Key 16:
Enchant for What You Don't Deserve

One of the great gifts of being a teacher is that you get to learn from your students. This is especially useful when your students take your teachings and find new framing to express them. A few years ago, my student Andrew Maxam threw down the glove to his fellow students in a way that struck me as particularly useful, and I have been repeating the challenge for myself ever since: "Conjure something that you want, but think you don't deserve."

I loved the idea so much, and it helped reframe my thinking to push myself farther as a Sorcerer and a person. I have expanded on it and included it here as our 16th Key.

Set Point Theory

In my book *Financial Sorcery*, I wrote about set point theory, which this key is closely tied to. In 1982, Dr. William Bennett and Joel Gurin were looking for an explanation as to why repeated dieting is unsuccessful in producing long-term change in body weight or shape. What they came up with is called "set point theory." According to this theory, there is a control system built into every person dictating how much fat he or she should carry—a kind of thermostat for body fat. Some individuals have a high setting whereas others have a low one. Whatever attempts at dieting are made will revolve around the gravity of this set point. Though Bennett and Gurin were speaking about a physiological process related to weight, psychologically speaking, we have all have set points for everything from health to wealth to love partners to spirituality.

Most of us have a surprisingly firm set point regarding our station in life. We get programmed to expect certain things. No matter what we say we want, we tend to gravitate to those expectations. This field of gravity is more difficult to escape than you might think. No matter what we may want, somewhere deep in the mind is a nagging thought of what we are "supposed to have" or what we "deserve." If we fall below these points, we enter into mental distress because things are not as they should be. If, however, we begin to rise far above the set point, we begin to get dizzy at this new height and again experience distress. What if we cannot maintain it? What if we fail? What do we do at this level? And so we gravitate back down to our nice, comfortable set point.

Ever hear someone say, "She's out of my league?" She wasn't. He just thought she was because his set point was dictating what he thought he could and couldn't attain. Ever see Dennis and Elizabeth Kucinich? That, my friends, is a man who did not let his set point dictate what was possible as far as women who would be interested in him.

I wrote a whole book on financial Sorcery that devotes a long key to set points, so I won't harp on about wealth too much. Suffice to say that when you grow up in a neighborhood where everyone is poor and doing unskilled labor or just flat-out unemployed, it becomes normalized in your psyche. If you grow up in a blue-collar family where people held careers as plumbers and electricians, that becomes the goal post, and children who go on to pursue college often tell me about how they are razzed by their families and abandoned by friends who see them as elitists. You can move up the socioeconomic ladder and find the educated white-collar middle-class balk and bristle at those who live in the highest strata of society, the 1 percent. Such heights violate their set points. It works in the reverse as well. In a neighborhood where everyone's parents are lawyers, doctors, or bankers, the child who wants to become an artist is seriously attacking his set point and will have it assaulted by those around him as well.

We even play this game with ourselves about our spirituality. There is a story about the great Tibetan master Milarepa being questioned by his students about his former lives. Milarepa was known to manifest many different Magical powers that defied explanation. Because of his Magical and spiritual attainments, his students figured that he must have been someone important in a previous life. They insisted he tell them what siddha or powerful Buddha he was in his past lives, or what *yidam* or spiritual power he was an emanation of. Milarepa scolded them for not having faith in the path, because if they did, they would realize that you do not have to be someone special from birth; anyone who followed the path could attain Buddhahood in this very life. This, however, was a violation of these followers' spiritual set point. They were comfortable following someone else, not being Buddhas themselves.

We often assume that great realization and Magical power is reserved for those who are born into it, those who *deserve* it. Some believe that Magic can only be really done if you are born with a caul, the seventh son of a seventh son, or born on a Magical date like St. John's Eve. Some believe that enlightenment is reserved for Saints and siddhas. But the Saints and siddhas assure us that enlightenment and Magic are, in fact, for us.

So whatever it is that you are working on, you should know that you probably have a set point that has been established by the circumstances of your birth, appearance, upbringing, and luck. In *Financial Sorcery*, I provide a ritualized moving of this set point, but it's really just a matter of reinforcing and achieving the new set point and holding it for a while until it becomes normal. You can ritualize it if you like, but it's perhaps better just to do it.

The first time I ever had $10,000 sitting in an account that was not immediately meant for something else, it blew me away. I felt discomfort just from having that fifth digit appear in my bank balance. I decided at that moment that was my new set point, and any time it dipped below that, I would feel an urgent discomfort that comes from dipping below where you should be. I have moved that point and others a few times now, but there is a difference between moving a set point and blowing it to smithereens. This section of the book is about advancing forward in our work, so let's blow stuff up!

Set Point Sacrilege

I will again quote Andrew:

> Maybe it's a raise that you think you haven't worked for, or the attention of someone special that you think is out of your league, or just some fun or pretty gift you'd like to give yourself. This has been a pretty powerful mental short-circuit trick for me; a lot of the time I get distracted by thoughts of whether or not I've

"earned" (in mundane or spiritual terms) the result that I'm summoning. Doing this every once in a while helps me remember that it doesn't really matter who "deserves" success or not. What matters is whether we make it happen for ourselves.

For people who are ostensibly dedicated to causing change through the radically strange and subtle methods of Sorcery, I am amazed at how many of us are trapped by ideas of what they do and don't deserve. I say "us" because I was once one of these people myself. Sorcerers who turn to the Gods and spirits to tell them what they deserve and don't deserve are hardly Sorcerers at all.

Let's be blasphemously blunt: Screw what you deserve or don't deserve. Just go get it because you want it.

No faux cosmic "it is my true will" justification; go for it just because you want it.

Don't invent some reason you "need" it to justify it. Just do it because you want it.

If there is some kind of karmic-rewards point system that monitors what people get based on what they deserve, trust that it is far too complicated for our slightly evolved monkey brain to figure out, and assume that if you want it, and it's not going to directly hurt anybody, it's okay to go for it.

If you are concerned about God or Gods having a destiny for you, then let them worry about that. Assume that your desire for a car with third-row seating is in fact part of that plan and let them tell you otherwise.

I am not saying to just do whatever you want and screw the consequences. That's a whole other ball of wax. This is not a license to screw people over, swindle your neighbors, or in any way rampage through the world less ethically than you normally would. You don't need to. Be honest, but be bold and go for what you want, whether you think you deserve it or not.

I am also not saying to drain your bank account for crap you can't afford. This is *not* about treating yourself because you deserve it. Going for something that you don't feel you deserve entails making yourself worthy of having that thing and able to possess it. If you just run out and spend the mortgage money on Occult books, that is not enchanting for what you don't deserve; it is acting stupid because you think you do deserve it.

This key is about blaspheming against the very idea that you do or don't deserve *anything*. Like reciting the Lord's Prayer backward, you are not moving your set point anymore; you are denying it actively and reclaiming its power as your own.

We're Not Worthy

Among some people who work the system outlined in Geoff Cobb's classic *New Avatar Power*, there are those who claim that the ritual invoking the spirit Elubatel has turned their lives upside down because they are not worthy of the success that they asked for. This hasn't happened to me with that system, but Jophiel once told me something similar when I was doing a success working for myself. "You are not worthy," he said. Rather than bow my head and accept this as a judgment of my personal worth, I questioned him further. What does "not worthy" mean? How do I become worthy? It turned out the issue really was not about any kind of moral worth but was instead a matter of arranging my life to be able to handle the gift I was asking for.

In my case, I was asking for a large increase in wealth, but my life was not set up to accommodate its manifestation in any reasonable way: I worked one job with set hours, fixed salary, and nowhere in the company to get promoted to. There was no other reasonable means for money to come in. I would end up just like Harold the Sorcerer in Key 6, working twice as many hours.

This is the type of situation that is a recipe for disaster: With no smooth channel for Magic to manifest through, it will either fizzle or, if pursued with enough vigor, cause the money to come in through insurance payments on a wrecked car, disability payments for your lost limb, or perhaps the cliché inheritance from a wealthy relative that just happened to die.

If you want to be "worthy" of big success, you have to make room for it. Part of this is making your life enchantable, as we spoke about in the 3rd Key, but another part is scalability. You have to have a life that is scalable to the effect you wish to achieve. Gordon White once wrote in his Rune Soup blog a few years ago: "There is a natural cap to the amount of money a baker can make.... It's the amount he can produce in an hour times the amount of hours he can physically work times the maximum amount people are willing to pay for bread before they say 'Fuck this, I'll buy it at the supermarket.'...Successful Magic requires scalability."[1]

This scalability is a kind of worthiness. You are showing that you have a life that can accommodate the blessing you are asking for. If you have a cup that holds 8 ounces but request 10 ounces of nectar, you are unworthy of receiving it. It doesn't say anything about you personally or morally—only that you need to go get a bigger cup!

Now, perhaps some powers do make moral judgment about people and whether they will work for them or not. If they sense the type of greed that not only desires for you to have more but for others to have less, perhaps that is a turn off to some powers—but you can always contact other powers. Just like people, you can always find someone willing to do it.

Tips for Blasphemy

When you enchant for something that somewhere deep down you feel you don't deserve, you are committing blasphemy against your lot in life. How do we do this? We go *big*.

Instead of asking how you can increase your customer count by 30 percent, ask how you can multiply it tenfold. What would you have to do to make yourself ready to play at this level? If you can figure out how to make yourself ready to receive that level of increase, then chances are you also know what to do to achieve that level of success. Start slinging those spells!

Instead of asking yourself if you can lose 20 pounds, ask what you would have to do to get into the best shape of your life. The very fact that it is hard might just inspire you to do more than just dropping the 20 pounds. Sometimes a difficult goal inspires us in a way that a simple goal does not.

Instead of hoping for some peace and centeredness from your meditation or spiritual practice, ask what your life would look like if you truly lived with one foot in the world of spirit or the divine. What would a life like that look like? Do you deserve such a life? It doesn't matter. Go for it anyway.

Magic is not alimony; it is not there just to keep you in the manner to which you have become accustomed. Use it to do the things that you never thought possible. The things that you feel you don't deserve.

The Take-Away

The problem we are solving here is self-limitation through a sense of what we deserve, or worse, what we think the Gods and spirits think we deserve. I don't care if Harold wants a golden chamber pot and neither do the spirits. I don't care if you want either! Just because someone's "norm" is making $300,000 a year does not make them more deserving than someone making $30,000. Free yourself of this burden.

The solution is simply to do it. Make sure that your life is set up to handle it, then pull the trigger and go for what you do not deserve. You have no lot in life other than what you accept and what you can grab.

Key 17:
Work Outside the Columns

odern Magic and Occultism has a terrible habit of creating neat little boxes to lock away all the spirits, Gods, planets, and powers that we deal with. There is nowhere you see this more clearly than in the columns of Khabbalistic Correspondences in Aleister Crowley's "777" or Donald Michael *Kraig's Modern Magick*. You see it in paganism as well: Aphrodite is the Goddess of Love, Mars of war, Jupiter of wealth. Even in the Church, this over-categorization plays out with the Saint of this or that being approached within a very narrow parameter.

There is nothing inherently wrong with this. It's a fine way to learn the basics and get the lay of the land. But this section of the book is all about moving your practice forward, and there is nothing more important for that than taking these powers out of their boxes and learning how widely they can be used. Don't let the columns become bars of a cage. Work outside them.

It's Not What You Know, It's Who

What if I told you the best spirit for a given task is not the one that is listed in the column that fits your problem, but the one that you have the strongest relationship with? How would that change your Magic?

Putting this into more mundane terms, let's pretend you are moving and need help. You can hire movers, but that would stretch you budget thin and you can't really afford it. There is a guy at work that looks like he would be able to haul boxes aplenty, but you have never spoken to him before. Your best friend would be glad to help, and you would probably have a great time while doing the work, but he is nowhere near as strong as that dude at work. Who do you ask? Your friend, of course! And guess what? When you do, maybe he has a hand-truck that will let you approach the move in a different way than you thought.

Now imagine that you are a devotee of Aphrodite and perform daily prayers and weekly offerings to her. You have received deep messages from her and established a strong relationship. When seeking a promotion at work, who do you turn to? Most column-based systems will tell you that

Zeus or Helios are the right Gods to invoke. The problem is that maybe you have never worked with Zeus, and Helios and Aphrodite don't get along at all.[1] I would work with Aphrodite, because the Goddess you know is better than the one you don't. Rather than ask simply to get promoted to higher office, something clearly Jupiterian, I would ask that she charm those who are making the decision and make them enchanted with your work and deservedness for the position. Maybe then I would perform micro-enchantments and invoke the aid of Zeus as her Father to bolster my leadership abilities, and appeal to Mercury so that the right people see the right things at the right times, but the macro-enchantment would be under the power of Aphrodite because she is who I already have a good rapport with.

Even though he is not a "Saint of Money," St. Cyprian has given me one of the best pieces of advice I ever received on financial Magic, to enchant for money left over after expenses rather than a simple number. I only received this piece of advice after working with him every Saturday for years and establishing a solid line of communication. Likewise, Astaroth is not widely thought of as a demon that heals, but she has aided me in a desperate situation precisely because I have a pact with her that goes all the way back to my first successful evocation nearly 30 years ago.

Hack the Planets

Astrologers and Sorcerers are both concerned with the planets and their influences but often in ways that seemingly contradict each other. Pure Astrological Magic is based on timing operations to coincide with optimal moments when the planets and stars best reflect the goal of the operation. You form a company, propose marriage, or create your talisman at the precise moment that the stars are aligned best for what you want to do. In the case of the astrological talisman, you are taking a sort of snapshot of the moment and infusing that energy into the talisman so that it broadcasts that power whenever it is worn or worked.

The Sorcerer, however, has to compensate for problems as they arise and cannot always wait for a perfect moment. This is especially true when the problems are not yours, but someone else's. If you are a Sorcerer worth your salt, your regular practices of offerings, devotions, and other daily work has your day-to-day life running fairly smoothly. However, the client is, by definition, a person with a problem that needs to be solved. What do you do when the planetary alignments are not perfect for what you want to accomplish? Hack the planets!

If you have ever seen those life-hacking articles about using toilet paper rolls to boost the bass on your phone, or using ketchup bottles for pancake batter, you know that with a little ingenuity you can sometimes expand your use of things well beyond what most people would consider. The planets are not different.

The biggest single thing that you can do to take advantage of the planets during times that might seem difficult to achieve your goal is to be flexible in your thinking about how other planets in a better aspect might be used to achieve the same result. The variety and fullness of each planet is unfortunately lost on most Magicians, and this is an area where a little study of traditional astrology would pay off.

Most Occultists have an appallingly simple idea of the powers of the planets that goes something like this:

- ⊛ **Moon:** sex and dreams and astral.
- ⊛ **Mercury:** intelligence and movement.
- ⊛ **Venus:** love and sex.
- ⊛ **Sun:** inspiration and health.
- ⊛ **Mars:** war and killing.
- ⊛ **Jupiter:** wealth and expansion.
- ⊛ **Saturn:** death and restriction.

This leads to very limited thinking. Everyone that needs money goes to Jupiter like he is their dad giving them money to go out on a Saturday night. If people want Love Magic they go to Venus, as if there are no reasons for their lack of companionship beyond not having enough Venus mojo. When people feel threatened, they go to Mars to kick butt, as if this is the only tool that a soldier has. Many Sorcerers I meet won't touch Saturn with a 10-foot wand for any reason at all, more afraid of its malefic influence than any demon they might summon.

The truth is that all seven planets can be called upon to affect just about any situation; you just have to know how to apply them.

To make sure students learn to be flexible with the planets, I have laid down what I call the Strategic Sorcery Two Week Challenge. This challenge encourages Sorcerers to start a working on a Monday and invoke a planet to impact their situation every *other* day for two weeks. Because each day is associated with a planet, and the arrangement of the planets through the week is according to the law of harmonic 5ths, a pattern where you do a work every other day lets you hit all seven planets on their appropriate day in the Chaldean order: Moonday, Wednesday (Mercury), Friday (Venus), Sunday, Tuesday (Mars), Thursday (Jupiter), and finally Saturday.

Let's take a look at some different scenarios and see how the planets can impact each, when it comes to either business or love.

In the Lunar sphere for business, you can invoke her to help make sure that you are working in alignment with the tides of commerce, affecting the deep minds of customers with a new marketing campaign, or revealing deception from backstabbing partners, bosses, and coworkers.

Next, we call upon Mercury to make sure that the motion is on your side. There is nothing more key when it comes to financial Magic. People treat money Magic as a static goal or set number, but there is never stasis in the business of personal finance; if you are not moving forward, you are moving backward. If your money is not moving around and making more money, then it is probably losing value, even if it is just sitting there under your mattress.

Venus is all about relationships. Have you ever been involved in a business venture that did not involve other people? Me neither.

The Sun is Gold, right? But it's also about inspiration and illuminating new ideas. No idea, no product. It's worth noting that while Jupiter is king of the Gods, the planets all revolve around the Sun. This is important for leadership and visibility.

Of course, you can call upon Mars to overcome competition, but I have had a lot of success drawing upon Mars for discipline and drive as well. Never underestimate the power of drive and discipline for finance. There is a reason that so many businessmen love *The Art of War*.

Jupiter is a no-brainer: expansion, governance, accretion, benevolence, etc. This is the one everyone calls on, so let's leave it at that.

That just leaves spooky Saturn. Everybody fears Saturn, and in traditional astrology, it is a great malefic, but limits are important. Jupiterian expansion needs the limits and strictness of Saturn to keep it focused, to make sure that systems do not expand unchecked. Think about all that Solar flare and Jupiterian expansion as an explosion. Saturn is like the barrel of a gun that can restrict it and make sure it hits a target. Also, very simply, if you want something to happen, you can use Saturn to restrict the opposite from happening.

So, if you are in a situation where Jupiter is negatively afflicted in your chart, or working during a time when Jupiter is retrograde or otherwise not aligned well, you have a lot of other options as a Sorcerer who is looking to make some business-enhancing spells. Just avoid the negatively affected planets that would ordinarily be concerned with business and take the others out of the box.

Let's take a look at love work: Luna is all about the love—deep mind, sexual drives. Not exactly stretching our minds with this one, so we can move on and pretend she is ill-afflicted and won't be available to help us this week.

You can call on Mercury to make yourself witty, confident, and funny. Looks may be the thing that gets initial attention, but wit, confidence, and humor will beat looks for sealing the deal and establishing a real connection every time. Mercury can also do some networking to make sure you are in the right room with Mr. or Ms. Right.

Venus is the love Goddess, and thus the obvious choice we do not need to go on about.

Sol will illuminate you and let you shine bright amongst dimmer lights. Honestly, I wonder why more Solar Love talismans are not in production.

Martial power might seem like a stretch for love work until you realize just how much there is to be conquered in the pursuit of love. Historically, the language of love draws upon the imagery of the hunter and prey, or frames love as a conquest, to the point where it is so common that it is cliché.

There is also an enormous amount of fear for people to overcome in the quest for love. Fear of rejection, fear of failure, fear of ridicule—the drives of love and sex are so primal that they turn the volume up on everything and make it impossible for us to keep our cool. One of the most successful love spells I ever did for a client was a Mars spell to overcome fear of rejection and build confidence. All the Venus work in the world did him no good until he got that under control. It was Aries, after all, that Aphrodite had the passionate affair with.

Has anyone in the Greek pantheon had more sex than Zeus? Jupiter is really good for love Magic. Having money doesn't hurt, either, for that matter.

Saturn is tricky, even when thinking outside the box. It can be used to end bad relationships, deal with pain, and, in general, get right with time—all things are impermanent. You can also petition the planet to remove its influence and free you from its grip. People rarely think about that, but it works. Petitioning a power to leave you alone is actually one of the oldest uses for Magic.

More nefarious Sorcerers might invoke Saturn in love spells that strongly bind someone or curse them until they love you. Such work is traditional in many circles, but that still doesn't make it a good idea.

We can take a quick look at healing too. Healing is often done with the Sun, but it's easy to see how Luna might work on mental anguish. Mercury can move you toward good health. Venus can heal emotions. Mars can do battle with disease directly. Jupiter encourages sovereignty over your own body and healthy vigor. Saturn might be petitioned to bind and control symptoms, or even give more time in terminal cases.

Learn to think differently about how to use the powers you have and you will never...

Be a One-Trick Pony

When I decided to study Tibetan Magic, I made myself a promise that other than group rites with friends, I would do *only* Buddhist Magic for five years. This was not asked of me; it was a limitation I put on myself so that I could focus on the system and learn it from its own base.

The problem was the only initiation I had for the first couple years was Vajrakilaya—the practice of destroying obstacles with the Phurba. I did not yet know how to do Kurukulla pujas to enchant people, Simhamukha for reversing harm, Manjushri for intelligence, or Dzambhala for building wealth. I had my Phurba and a couple weeks retreat of how to use it. So I became a one-trick pony for a while.

Need protection? Let's destroy the obstacle with Phurba! Need money? Let's destroy your poverty with Phurba! Need love? Let's destroy the obstacle to finding love with Phurba! Calcified gland? Let's Phurba the heck out of that! Bad weather on the way? Point the Phurba at the cloud and PHAT! Whatever it was, I found a way to apply the Phurba to the problem.

Two things happened. First, I learned how to think outside the box of what I could and couldn't do with a Magical nail. Second, I got *really* good at using Phurbas for Magic. Taking one deity, Saint, or practice, and restricting yourself to just that for a year or two is a worthwhile thing I recommend you do at some point. You will learn that you apply your Magic in a variety of ways, while getting really great at what you have specialized in.

The Take-Away

What this key is telling you is to look at the powers that you interact with in a different way. I could have talked about the Elements or the Saints instead of Gods and planets but the lesson would be the same: What powers are you close to? What forces are most available right now? How can you apply them differently?

What powers are local? That is another factor to consider. The Tenma sisters were bound by Padmasambhava at the Asura Cave in Nepal, and when I was at that cave, I felt their presence immediately. Here in America, they seem more distant than the Yakshinis that dwell in the land where I live.

For good or for ill, Harold has a relationship with Salphegor even though the Grimoire lists Salphegor as a wealth-granting spirit. Sal points out that money has never hurt anyone's chances with the finding partners— a fact that seems to be true for both men and women and hetero and homosexual couples. Money has no biases. Whatever powers you decide to call upon, how can you use them in ways that are different from how you typically think of them? This is how great and interesting works of Magic are made.

Key 18:
Failing Without Flailing

In Key 7, I told the story about my friend's store that was failing and how we conjured Tzadkiel to save it. Tzadkiel was not able to save the business as it existed, but was able to limit losses for my client and extract her from a situation that could have ended much, much worse. In that key, it was an example of how using Sorcery only when things are already an emergency limits your options. In this key, it is an example of accepting defeat with skill and positioning yourself for a fall: failing without flailing.

The Tower and The Star

When I read cards, I never read just one in isolation. Just as you need at least two words to work a sentence, I need at least two to show how to move from one state to another. The pair of La Maison Dieu and the Star is one that comes up when people need to let go of trying to fix

everything, and instead should focus on letting it crash and burn in a controlled way.

One of the dangers of Sorcery that people don't think about is the ability to perpetuate a bad status quo with the power of Magic. It's just as dangerous as a demon or psychic attack. These are the reasons I say that emergency Magic can be very bad Magic. The job you hate, the relationship that is dead at the core, the place that you live in but cannot afford anymore—there are some situations that Magic cannot fix outright, but instead perpetuate for years on end—putting off the hard fall that eventually lets you regroup and do something even better.

A much better option sometimes is to use Magic to control the fall, so that we wind up minimizing damage, recovering quicker, and opening new opportunities.

In La Maison Dieu, we have the blasted tower and the two figures falling head on into the ground from the blasted tower. So what can we do?

Look at Le Toille. The two falling people have become the water in the jars. They are still going to wind up on the ground, but instead of falling, they are being poured out. It's a controlled event. They get to flow rather than splat.

The tower itself becomes the woman in the card. Is she a Goddess that you invoked to help deal with the situation? Is she simply the fact that when you acknowledge and plan for something, you at least have *some* influence as to how it happens?

Then I send them the canned response that I do not work in that field. If pressed, I will recommend someone who does, even though it's probably not a good idea.

Magic designed to force people to love you, sometimes by any means necessary, is present if not prevalent in pretty much all cultures. Buddhists are not beyond it and there are spells in the *Arya Tara Kurukulla Kalpa* for binding lovers and gaining the affections of important people. There are defixiones tablets from as late as the 6th century to Hekate, aimed at binding specific women to fall in love with the caster. There are spells that involve Saints like Magdeline and Bartholomew for stirring love in a target as well. There are spells in the books attributed to St. Cyprian for binding lovers, which is ironic because Cyprian himself became a Christian when Justina rebuked his Magic aimed to enslave her with love by making the sign of the cross.

People feel so passionate about getting or keeping the object of their affections that there are actually Love Curses. Probably the most popular is the summoning of the "Intranquil Spirit," or sometimes the "Seven Intranquil Spirits" that will torture your target until they come to you. These spirits, that tradition holds are in Hell, are asked to "Capture the five senses of (name of target). To disturb him, and dominate him, and not let him have peace."[1]

Do you remember the Astronaut Diaper Drive of 2007? She was an astronaut who was found with a steel mallet, a buck knife with a four-inch blade, a BB gun, and a map to her lover's house in her car. She was famously wearing a diaper because, well, who has time to stop for the bathroom when true love is on the line and you are heading to Florida to tie it up with duct tape?

When you are sitting down to do a spell, or hiring someone to do a spell, that involves getting a specific person to love you no matter what, to get them to love you *or else*, *you* are that astronaut.

It *is* traditional for sure, but when you consider how dependent women were on men for resources in the past, and how many men run off with younger women when the going gets tough—you can see why these spells might be justifiable in such places and times. But if you are reading this book, you are probably not in such a time and place. The people who make these requests are largely doing it out of obsession, not necessity.

That is your clue that you should let it go, whether it is an unrequited love interest, a business that you have sunk so much money into that you don't want to admit it's failing,[2] or a court case that is not going to pan out. Know when to cut your losses and move on. Don't be the diaper-wearing astronaut.

"I Meant to Do That!"

Remember in *Pee-wee Herman's Big Adventure* when he wiped out doing a trick on his bike, but sprung right up again and said "I meant to do that!" Be like Pee-wee! Back in my early 20s, my life was kind of coming apart at the seams. I was living with a girlfriend and two other friends from high school in a row house in Trenton, New Jersey. My girlfriend had broken up with me, but we still lived in the same house, which is never fun. I crashed my car, again, and could no longer afford the insurance to stay on the road; in New Jersey, this is also not fun. On top of that, my roommates had just discovered a love of indoor fireworks, not the Elvis Costello metaphorical kind, but literally shooting off fireworks inside the house and out the window. I was fairly certain that our neighbors, who we didn't like at all, were soon going to kill us in our sleep. That would not be fun either. It was my first living situation after leaving home, and it was not going well.

I could have fought on, but instead I decided to call it quits. I stopped all the Magic I had going aimed at getting the girl back, finding money for the car insurance, and getting my roommates to stop blowing stuff up and just let it go. I let it all fall, because it was going to fall anyway eventually.

There was really no way around the car issue at this point, so I got on the phone with Matt, our illustrious illustrator, who I thought would make a better roommate. I needed to get out before my roommates literally blew up the house so we created a servitor to find an apartment in Center City, Philadelphia. No need for a car when you live in the middle of the city. We created the servitor at his apartment and just walked around the neighborhood that we wanted to live in. At one moment, we both saw a sort of shimmering presence on a building that we took to be our servitor, so we called the number of the realty office and voila, we found our apartment!

I made and offering to Papa Legba to help me find a job and new friends in the city, and went in the next day, just two weeks before moving in. That day I met Gendler, who was at that time literally the best possible person in the city to meet, because not only could he help me copy my resume and put the word out on a job, but he also knew every Occultist in the city. Within a week, I had a job lined up. Problem #2 now solved.

The girl problem would stay waiting for a bit as I dated for a couple years, but I eventually made an offering to Erzuli Freda on a street corner and shortly thereafter stopped living with Matt and moved in with the person who eventually agreed to marry me. The Erzuli offering was a little half-assed, as it was really in a style that would be more appropriate to an offering to Pomba Gira, but it worked, and an ironwork veve of Erzuli hangs over our bed to this day.

Some of the very best things I have in life—many of my best friends, my experiences in Thelesis Camp, my studies in Tibetan Buddhism, my time living with my best friend, and my wife—are the direct result of letting something that was going to fall apart fall with some skill and controlled descent.

The Take-Away

The problem is that no matter how great we are at Magic, we cannot control everything. If we use Magic to prolong our situation, we just delay the inevitable and make the fall harder. If we deploy increasingly intense Magic because we are obsessed, we become like Harold in the cartoon on page 179 and go too far. Listen to Salphegor and just let it go.

It's better to perform divinations to see the outcome with and without Sorcerous intercession. Ask yourself, "Am I hanging on to this because I believe in what I am doing and think it will work out, or am I hanging on out of obsession or refusal to let go of sunk costs?"

Perform what Stoics call a Premeditatio Malorum: a meditation on the worst-case scenario that could result from letting things collapse. If you have decided to let things go, ask yourself:

Is there anything from this that I can salvage and retool into a new shape that might make a difference?

- ✪ If not, what are the things you need to have in place to move on from here?
- ✪ What preparations do you need to make to deal with the worst-case scenario?
- ✪ What Sorcery can you do to help make sure the worst-case scenario does not come to pass?

This should give you the clarity you need to enchant your way into a better future.

Key 19:
Know Where Your
Scarcity Lies

Magic is, and should be, a spiritual pursuit. People who call themselves Magicians are concerned solely with spiritual evolution. They walk the paths of the Tree of Life, invoke angels to teach divine knowledge, and sometimes initiate in Magical orders promising self-transformation. Many who call themselves Witches are interested in it as a religion, celebrating sabbats, and communing with old Gods for a sense of well-being and fulfillment, as well as a mystic path. I describe myself as a Sorcerer because while I have a deep interest in mysticism, I let the light of spirit shine through me outwardly in the form of spells that I put into the world. There is no mistaking that a Sorcerer does spells and is out there making things happen with Sorcery.

In this book, there are stories of enchanting for money, love, sex, protection, and healing. We enchant to address scarcity. Many people, especially those who only do emergency Magic, experience scarcity for the same things. The reason I wrote this book is to help get you past that point. But that doesn't mean that scarcity goes away—it just changes.

Money and Time

When you are starting out as an adult, you have a shortage of money, but lots of time. During this period, a DIY mentality serves you well: from mundane tasks like repairing your own plumbing and fixing your car, to Magical tasks like making your oils and Magical tools from scratch. You might be joining an order or taking classes on work-study rather than paying for them outright.

As you get older, you become more successful and money stops being in short supply. Unfortunately, people at this stage start to face a deficit of time. Careers, kids, community involvement, and advancing your passions make it impossible keep up with the demands. Suddenly you realize time is the scarcity rather than money. In a way, this is a worse situation, because time is not a renewable resource. You can make more money, but there's not much you can do about time.

Suddenly it makes sense to pay someone else to fix the sink and make your oils and tools. Yet people do not recognize this shift in scarcity and try to do everything themselves, focusing on getting more and more money instead of increasing the amount of time they have available.

If they recognized the scarcity shift, they might invoke Saturn instead of Jupiter so they can start streamlining what they do and make the same amount of money in less time. They might go to a Kalachakra empowerment or start working with a deity like Aeon or Zurvan to set them right with the rhythms of time. I invoked the Gnostic deity Abrasax for this years ago, and my life improved drastically. His name works out to be 365 according to gematria, and he oversees the turning of the stars and planets. His laughter created time itself. Though the original working was quite elaborate, I refresh it occasionally by reciting the word *ablanathanalba* 365 times—a time saver!

Time and Attention

Hopefully you get your time whipped into shape. You streamline your life so that business, family, and personal time are in good balance. Now your problem is attention: Even with maximized time and infinite money, you cannot give attention to everything, so where do you place it? Attention is a resource just like time and money, and it must be used wisely.

I talk to students who tell me they don't have time to do 100 mantras to Hekate a day, or to make offerings, or start a side business. These are often the same people I see spending hours debating politics on Facebook and who are passionate fans of literally every sci-fi or fantasy television show out there. These folks are not facing a scarcity of time; they are facing a scarcity of attention.

The Magic for addressing attention scarcity is not as easy as a few spells. I recommend meditation and self-examination more than anything. A good system of prioritizing tasks also helps. I use Zen To Done, which is a scaled-down version of David Allen's Getting Things Done system. Whatever tools you use, they should help you keep your attention on what is important, rather than what is momentarily distracting.

One piece of Magic I can recommend is to start every day by invoking the powers of the planet of that day. I focus on the Archangels, but you can easily adopt the practice for Greek, Babylonian, or Norse Deities who have all been associated with days of the week. This kind of day-to-day invocation helps place the day into focus and keep your timing solid.

As you look at where your attention lies, you decide to drop or minimize things that effect other people. You are bound to piss people off when you withdraw or do not give as much of your bandwidth as they would like. There are some things that, left to my own devices, I would not want to focus my attention on, but are important to my family or close friends, so I do it anyway. This is not a waste. This is giving.

Attention and Energy

Got money, time, and attention under control? Are you exhausted? Full lives *are* exhausting. Now your scarcity shifts to energy. Energy is a renewable resource. Non-Magical solutions come first: sleep, exercise, diet. Paying attention to this holy trinity of energy management gives you a good basis upon which to build. Any energy-increasing strategy that involved Magic, but not these three factors, is built on a shaky foundation and unlikely to succeed.

Once you have those under control, you can think about setting your rhythms for the day. There is evidence that scheduling your day around your ultradian rhythms keeps you energized. These are periods of high energy and productivity that last around 90 minutes followed by a break of about 20 minutes. If you can manage your day around this cycle, you will hold your energy, attention, and time in harmony better than if you work against it.

Other Types of Scarcity Shifts

Because money is something we deal with regularly, I use it for examples when I talk about Sorcery and, in this case, the scarcity shifts that come after your finances are under control. There are other types of scarcity that you can and should think about addressing, with or without Magic.

Because of the advent of smartphones, we are the first generation in history to have a scarcity of idle time. We listen to podcasts when we drive, we look at emails when we wait in line, and we post photos of our food to Facebook instead of sitting down and enjoying a meal. If you follow the advice of previous sections in this key, you might think I want you to kill idle time, but nothing could be further from the truth. It is vital for the mind to have time when it is awake but able to drift and play. These are the windows that insight and genius arise within, as well as the moments when omens and subtle forces might be perceived.

Remember the pick-up artist movement from years ago? Love them or hate them, these guys excelled at getting girls. Keeping a relationship, however, was not their forte. What do you do after your love spells have worked? You need to find what is scarce in your relationship and conjure that instead. What builds a strong relationship is often very different than what attracts people to us initially. Understanding, openness, communication—these things can be enchanted for just as well as finding love. Sadly, the amount of requests to make talismans of communication between partners is nowhere as high as the requests to bind lovers out of obsession. If there was more of the former, there might be less need for the latter.

It's no secret that as we get older, our health deteriorates. There is a good chance that if we used Magic to build financial success, start families, and work for causes we support, we have increased the stressors in our life and are speeding that deterioration up! Even if you have never had serious health issues, with every passing year, it becomes an increased scarcity that you may want to address. We know emergency response Magic is not as good as emergency prevention Magic. Nowhere is this truer than with our health.

The Take-Away

Why am I pointing this out? Because if you are like me, your passion for Sorcery and the Occult is so strong that it creates an added draw of money, time, attention, energy, and other resources far beyond what most people experience.

Too many wealth Sorcerers focus on money when what they need is better management of time, awareness, and energy. Too many Sorcerers throw out love spells when what they need are spells to help them grow and communicate with a partner. Figure out where the real poverty lies. Focus on where you need the help and launch your spells at that.

In the last comic, Harold was ready to use aggressive love Magic to keep his girlfriend. Now that he let her go, he thinks another love spell will solve his problems, but he doesn't know where his scarcity lies. Finding partners is not where his shortage is; it's in his charm and listening skills.

Key 20:
Trade In Goals
for Trajectory

L ast year, I did a consultation for a client who wanted to increase her income. Before the consultation, I asked her to tell me what she wanted. The goal she named was "to make $20,000 per month in 2016." It fit the metrics of a good goal that I listed in Key 2. This would represent a significant uptick from her current income and was thus inspiring. It was not such an increase that it is unrealistic or unattainable given their business and what they brought in last year. It was not vague at all, and easily measurable. I am usually happy to get goals like this.

I had her re-frame her goal anyway.

I had been working with this person for a few years and decided that this goal was too static. In this case, January was already half over, and though her business has been steadily improving, she would not be likely, even with Sorcery, to hit the $20,000 mark that month, so she would be starting off the year already failing.

Let's imagine, though, that she did hit that goal in January. Does anyone really want to have the same goal 12 months later? What does that say about her business? It says that it has plateaued, that it is static and lost its momentum. This would be just as true for a relationship, for fame, or for spiritual growth as it is for business.

It was time for my friend to let go of goals and replace them with trajectory.

I told the client that making $240,000 that year was totally a great yearly goal, but that they should be sure to break it down so that they were hitting that $20,000-a-month mark in June or July rather than as a static sum. Aim for $15,000 in January, $16,000 in February, $17,000 in March, and so on. After the summer, they want to be making *more* than $20,000. In September, aim for $23,000. In December, aim for $24,000 or $25,000 for the month. This way, she hits the number she wants for the year and does not suffer from failing the first few months when an instant increase to $20,000 falls outside the *spectrum of enchantablity*. She had to tweak this strategy to accommodate her seasonal ups and downs, but eventually developed a great system.

The best part is that she set the trajectory for next year, which is the biggest benefit in this kind of thinking. She missed her yearly goal in

2016 by only $6,000, but was happy with the result anyway. The steady increase created a trajectory for where she wanted to head, and now she had a clearer vision of how she wanted 2017 to go.

When Goals No Longer Serve

At the beginning, there are always things to fix: the debt to pay down, the shitty job that is falling out from under you, maybe even a dangerous situation to escape from like an abusive partner, a court case, or someone threatening your safety.

Next come the things that are not emergencies but represent the basics of whatever you consider a happy life: a bachelor's or master's degree, a career you enjoy, a nice home in the country, an apartment in the city, a long-term partner, a kid or two. These milestones are important and are defined by static goals, a gold ring that you need to grab. They are the nouns in the sentences of life.

After you get these under wraps, what then? I suggest that it is time to stop focusing on the nouns of life and start thinking about the verbs. Think less about the next goal and more about the trajectory of your life.

This shifting in thinking solves two problems that I see when people get to this stage in their life: The first is that they find that having all the things they thought would make them whole and complete and happy do not in fact make them whole and complete and happy. The second is that, having attained a certain level of success, they feel like they are untouchable, and that things will stay this way forever—which of course they never do.

The Trajectory of Fulfillment

It's a funny thing. Happiness is often found in temporary things like a good shag, a night out with friends, or a particularly satisfying meal. This is why studies often show things like leather jackets and meaningless sex make people happier than having children. But is happiness the same as fulfillment? I don't think so. I think that though happiness can be found in these short-term pleasures, true joy comes from commitment and striving. Perfection is found in the go-getting rather than in just getting. It's a verb, not a noun.

Once you have that relationship in place, what then? Lots of married couples report that their partners stop striving to make their relationships better after marriage, as if that seal removes the need to think more about it. It doesn't though, which is why as soon as laws and societal norms allowed for divorce, people started divorcing in droves. If you set a trajectory for your partnership, you stop asking yourself whether you have it or not, and start asking about the strength of your partnership, the communication, the sex, and so on. Your marriage is not a static thing; it is in constant motion. Early in relationships, people often ask, "Where are we going with this?" but stop asking once the relationship becomes committed. If you think in terms of trajectory, that question never leaves your mind.

When I started working for myself, my big goal—the one that would define success for me—was to make $5,000 a month from my writing, teaching, and consulting. I actually had posted it to one of those "vision boards" and hung it in the office. The year that I finally had the bravery to quit my day job (which I would have been fired from soon anyway, because I spent more time writing blog posts and books than actually working), I hit that goal. If success was a goal, I grabbed it. The night that I filed the taxes for that year, I sat down with what I call my "board of directors," the spirits and deities I work with for my business success. They told me this was just the tip of what was possible and that if I dedicated myself to serving my readers and my students, I should stop thinking about a final number to maintain for a happy life and start thinking about percentage increases over the previous year. I am happy to report that the advice of my spirits[1] was wise indeed, and my set point has been moved again and again. Now, like the trajectory of a rocket, I have a plan for my continued rise, as well as slow descent for when I get very old. I will land when I'm dead.

Knowing that this journey doesn't end until I am dead is itself a source of joy. Sure, there are lots of goals to reach within that trajectory, but the outlook is very different than when my highest aspiration was to match what I was making at my day job. I now view this as a moving target.

Inescapable Impermenance

The other problem that trajectory thinking solves is thinking that once you are out of your time of difficulty and danger that you are somehow done. A few years ago, a good friend of mine, who is also a hell of a Magician, finally paid down all his debts and hit the six figure mark that he held in his mind as sort of the "end-all be-all" of financial success. He was so relieved that all this "was done." I said, "Done?" He assured me that yes, done. He didn't have to "worry" about that part of his life anymore.

It's five years later, and sadly, he is no longer at six figures. One of the people in his department that he trained was able to do what he did for a lot less money. He was not done, and if you are still breathing, neither are you. Neither am I.

The one thing that remains constant in life is change. When looking back over life, we can take a solid assessment of our success and failures, but when people project ahead, they often have an amazing blindness to the possibility of things going south. It is particularly hard when you are at the top of your game to see the ground slipping away from under your feet. A great example of this is Blockbuster Video.

Netflix was founded in 1998 around the same time that Blockbuster Video's initial public offering on the market was valued at $4.8 billion. In 2000, Blockbuster declined several offers to purchase Netflix for just $50 million. They were not interested in this scrappy company because they had just dominated the entire video market and felt invincible. They continued to feel invincible as the industry that they let slipped out from under them. In August of 2010, the same month that they were de-listed from the New York Stock Exchange, Kevin Lewis, the company's digital strategy head, explained to Fast Company that "We're strategically better positioned than almost anybody out there. Never in my wildest dreams would I have aimed this high."[2] One month later, Blockbuster filed for bankruptcy valued at just $14 million. The reason I am bringing this up is that Blockbuster was not thinking about an ever-moving, ever-shifting trajectory, but instead about static goals.

Life is a study in movement. Every person that has ever lived has died. Every company that was ever started will eventually close. Every empire that has ever risen will fall. Keep moving. Hold in your mind the one thing you can be sure of: If you are not growing, you are shrinking. There is no stasis.

Put more simply, don't sit on your ass when things are going well. Look at your trajectory and ask, "What's next?"

What Does Trajectory Thaumatury Look Like?

Bringing this back to the realm of practical Magic, what do spells for trajectory look like as opposed to spells for static goals?

The first element is that the spells are long term and the materia used is going to be based around something that you keep around, update, or change as your needs arise and move.

Full altars, of course, would be fantastic, if you have the space for them. It's great to keep a financial altar, a relationship altar, a security altar, and so on. You can burn candles for individual goals and obstacles on the bottom tier of the altar, while placing long-term items like statues and spirit fetishes on the upper tiers; that will keep everything tied to your overall trajectory. Unfortunately, we don't all have the space for multiple altars, and because life changes, we must never let our Magic be chained to such elaborate structures. Even I have space problems, and I do this for a living. When my twins passed their first birthday, I had to give up my room in favor of a smaller shrine in the garage until I could get a larger space. When I traveled for long periods of time, I had to do without altars entirely. Enjoy such elaborate set-ups while you can, but as one teacher once told me, "You should be able to continue your practice even if you found yourself in prison."

Spirit bottles require less space than a full altar. Filled with herbs and items that relate to both the spirit and the trajectory of the facet of life that they are overseeing, these bottles can be kept on a shelf. Think in terms of a permanent, oversized mojo hand. Place a candle in the top of the bottle and speak to the spirit when it is lit. Perhaps leave an offering on a plate that the bottle sits on. Tell the spirit how it's going and ask for advice and assistance. If necessary, update the items in the bottle, giving the spirit tools to evolve along with your life.

My client who I spoke about at the beginning of this key uses a spirit bottle now to help chart her trajectory. She has grown as much as she can on her own and now has to hire assistants, so she added gravel root, High John, and special consecrated hooks to the bottle to help find the right person to help her. Another client had to move his home-based business to an office, and now has added dirt from the new office to his bottle.

Petitions are my primary way of managing my trajectory. I make quarterly petitions about what I would like to see, and every equinox and solstice, I make an offering of thanks, burn the petition, and replace it with a new one under my loadstone. Some petitions are yearly instead of quarterly and are updated on the feast day of the Saint that I am petitioning. I then anoint it with oil as I make the offerings and place it under the statue, or inside of it if it has a drawer in the base.

The Jupiterian Cashbox I wrote about in *The Sorcerer's Secrets* is another method of keeping financial trajectory, and since that book came out, hundreds of students have sent me pictures of their own boxes filled with dirt from the key spots in their life, loadstones to attract increasing wealth, and of course money that goes into the box for a week, then gets taken out and spent.

I have now taken this idea a step further and made a round base box in which to place papers for investments I have made. In the box are items related to Helios and, in each direction, is an image of one of his horses.

The box is painted in gold leaf and I have asked Helios to keep my investments shining, to hold their worth overall, over time. I know that some will lose value, and at times they all will, but overall, I am trying to get a nine-percent annual return and doing well at it.

For other types of short-term investments, I have dedicated a statue of Baphomet and placed him over the petition. The choice of Baphomet is because of his arms: one points up and says "coagula," and the other points down and says "solve." This is a perfect metaphor for how this investment's trajectory is going to go, and I ask Baphomet to guide me and watch over these investments as they rise and fall, making sure that I pull out at an optimal time. It's still early in this experiment, but I am having fun with it.

Whatever tactics for trajectory you use, the key points are:

- ⊛ Open-ended rather than closed goals.
- ⊛ Thoughts expressed in terms of movement rather than stasis.
- ⊛ Recognition of the inevitability of change.

Even when you feel like you are at the top of your game and things have seemed to plateau into a nice rhythm for a few years, you are *still* in motion. Set your trajectory or it will be set for you.

Enlightenment as a Trajectory

This book is meant to be about practical Magic, but I hope you will indulge me on a bit of musing here on spiritual ascent and trajectory.

A lot of religions express their result in terms of hard goals. In Buddhism, for instance, enlightenment has very set definitions. Not all schools agree on what those definitions are, but the definitions within those schools are pretty set. In Christianity, there are characteristics of salvation as well as Gnosis. Most traditions have a goal that they have attempted to define as a final or ultimate state.

I have come to view spirituality as an open-ended trajectory. The goals within it are interesting signposts, but we may or may not wind up marching past those particular ones. For the most part, even if there is a final enlightenment or final Gnosis, we are so far from that, that we are better off just charting the next step of the journey and keeping the trajectory we want in mind. You can spend your time obsessing about whether the final enlightened state entails bliss and emptiness, or emptiness and clarity—or you can know that you are on a trajectory that improves clarity, kindness, power, and understanding, and worry about the next step in front of you.

Sadly, the history of religion is a study in people who argue and fight over what the final goal or ultimate nature of divinity is. There were once texts that were literally chained up in the bottom of the Potala Palace because they expressed a view of emptiness that the state disagreed with. Think about that: They chained up the texts.

During my many years communing with Hekate, I would press her for what the goal of all this Magic she was teaching me was. "To go beyond" was all she would say. Frustrated, I asked when it stops. When do we stop "going beyond"? When do we get to the destination?

The Goddess's reply was this: "I haven't yet. Why should you?"

The Take-Away

Harold has finally achieved a state of comfort. Money is good, love is good, and he wants it all to just stay like that. Our demon sadly cannot accommodate him. Change is the only constant in life.

No matter what you are attempting—weight loss, increase in clients, return on investments, or clarity of mind—remember to think in terms of trajectory and not static goals. Then, strategize accordingly. After you fix the things in your life that are broken and attain the basic milestones of a happy life, start thinking about trajectory rather than individual goals. Life is and always has been in motion. You need to think in verbs more than nouns.

Key 21:
Maintain Sovereignty

I think it's fair to say that many people consider Tibet a place that spent a lot of time and energy developing its spirituality and its Magic. While some of this reputation is pure fiction, Dr. Strange, Dr. Doom, The Shadow, and Mandrake all got their powers there after all, it can be said that Magic was integrated into everyday life, from medicine to even the government, and spirits are taken absolutely seriously.

While studying the fall of Tibet to the Chinese, I noted that a lot of the Oracles were telling the Dalai Lama to fight back. They recommended working with the CIA and foretold a glorious defeat of the Chinese. Obviously, this did not come to pass. When I asked my teachers why the Oracles were wrong, they shared a very old saying that I think is a good place to start our discussion of the 21st key:

 མི་ཕྱུག་ཐུག་ན་ལྷ་ལ་ཞུས། །ལྷ་ཕྱུག་ཐུག་ན་སྐྱག་རྫུན་བཤད། །

'u thug nas lha la dris/ lha 'u thug nas rdzun bshad

"When people are desperate they petition the Gods. When the Gods get desperate, *they lie*."

They are a lot like people in that respect. They tell the truth most of the time, but they can lie when they want and sometimes simply do not know. What better reason not to yield sovereignty over yourself?

You Are In Charge

Religion is very often in the business of blaming events on the will of the Gods. From the Plague of Thebes blamed on Ares, to televangelists claiming homosexuals caused Hurricane Katrina, and the governor of Tokyo blaming "national egotism" for the tsunami of 2011, there are always those who will blame events on the Gods and spirits. On the smaller scale of our personal lives, people do this as well. Just this week, one of my family members thanked God for steering Hurricane Irma west toward another city that, assumingly, God was less happy with.

If Magic and Sorcery is about anything, it is about taking charge of things ourselves and becoming an active participant in the play of providence. Rather than blaming the Gods for events, we attempt to get them to aid us. We are spirits, so we throw our own weight at the problem and ask the Gods for help. If we succeed, then we thank them. If we fail, then we don't.

We either accept the situation or we try again, but a Sorcerer should not simply leave it up to the Gods. Otherwise, what is the point of Sorcery at all?

The Spirits Do Not Micro-Manage

In Key 14, I mentioned a spell that I did when I first started teaching. The spell was an evocation of Tzadkiel that requested he help me build my business, to reach more people, and to make more money doing what I loved. Tzadkiel, in his otherworldly way, must have looked at my life like a mechanic looks at an engine and said, "Well, here's your problem right here! Just get rid of this other job that you don't really like, and you will have an extra 40 hours a week to devote to Strategic Sorcery! Let's just go ahead and take that out...." I was laid off from my day job shortly thereafter. The problem is, I needed that job to pay the bills.

Now, funny enough, a good friend, fellow author and Magician Rufus Opus was doing the same thing at around the same time. He *also* evoked Tzadkiel, and he *also* got laid off from his day job after requesting help getting his teaching off the ground. How and why this happened is where we differ. He feels that Tzadkiel knows the mechanics of the whole universe and loves us and knows what is best. Therefore, our respective lay-offs were the wisdom of the spirit.

I, however, do not share his faith. My feeling is that Tzadkiel doesn't live here on earth, is not human, and is not responsible for knowing every little tidbit about my life and how it works. I evoked him and bound him to a job, which he did with efficiency and speed. The fact that it got me laid off from another job that I needed was not his grand plan for my life; it was just a logical response to my request. But it also wasn't his fault—it was mine.

I am certain that it was not the will of God or the Archangel of Jupiter that I get laid off from a job, just to have a few more hours to devote to my business while frantically freaking out and finding a new day job that didn't pay as well as the one I lost, only to go and quit that job a few years later.

Rufus, however, is equally certain that it *was* divine will and we can call it a plan because we can both look back and say, "Well, if that didn't happen, maybe I would not be where I am today." That's true of anything, though, isn't it? Yes, things will work out in the end, but it's not because things work out according to some plan written by a detail-obsessed divine author of creation. It is because you will work out a new plan. You make yourself happy in the new situation and look back and say, "See, if it wasn't for this or that, I wouldn't be here." Well, yeah. But you would be somewhere else, probably just as happy if not more so.

Mechanisms of Magic

The biblical books of Samuel tell the stories of how people who aren't supposed to look into or touch the Ark of the Covenant are stricken dead by God. In 1 Samuel 6:19, the men of Beth Shemesh looked into the Ark and were stricken dead. Thankfully, Indiana Jones remembered this story and told Marion to close her eyes at the end of *Raiders of the Lost Ark*, thus sparing them both the Nazi face-melting treatment. In 2 Samuel 6:2, we learn of Uzzah, who was just trying to save the Ark from falling off the cart when the ox stumbled. Did God appreciate the effort? Nope. God struck him dead too. But was it really that God was mad at their irreverence? Or was it perhaps that they were not wearing all the priestly prophylactics like the breastplate that is needed to handle direct exposure to divinity? Might this have been less about God being pissed off and murderous than it was about these guys touching a live wire and getting electrocuted? That is my take on it.

In the New Testament, we have a more positive example of the mechanistic nature of divine power when a woman who had been bleeding for 12 years touched the hem of Jesus's garment. Jesus stopped and asked, "Who touched me?" When the disciples all denied it, he insisted, noting that "Someone touched me; I know that power has gone out from me." He didn't heal her by will. He healed her accidentally and drained power from him through touch. When she admits to touching him, he notes that her faith had healed her and sends her on her way. He didn't do it on purpose; he didn't even know she was there. It just happened because power moves like that.

My point in bringing up these biblical examples is to point out that the unseen forces of the world are, at least as far as I have found, much more mechanistic than most spiritual people believe. There is not a reason for everything and no one overseeing the unfolding of life in every detail. It is, in fact, this mechanistic nature that allows Magic to have an effect at all. If everything was pre-written, there would be no point to Sorcery. We could all just pray for what we hoped would happen, but ultimately it wouldn't matter.

Instead there are powers and spirits and forces that we get to communicate with and leverage. We are, in fact, one of these powers ourselves and must never forget it.

An Offering of "Thanks, but No Thanks"

Even if we accept that there is no divine plan or mechanistic universe, a lot of people feel that if a spirit or spell gives them a result, that they are committed to accepting that result and to do otherwise would be an offense against the Gods.

Wrong!

If you were looking for a date and I set you up with one of my friends, would you continue to date them and marry them just because I set you guys up? Of course not! So why do we feel we must do this with the spirits?

I have already shared the story in Key 15 about how Manman Brigitte got me a job offer at a hospital for the criminally insane. Was I obligated to take this job? Heck no! And I didn't take it. I considered this more a joke on her part than a serious attempt at solving my problem anyway— the Guédé are like that sometimes, and this was a kind of thing that they would do. Instead of making an offering of thanks for her boon, I made an offering of "thanks, but no thanks." I drew her veve, laid out the rum she likes, thanked her for her efforts, then let it go. If you work with spirits, I suggest you practice the offering of "thanks, but no thanks" on a regular basis. Just because your spell manifested something doesn't mean you have to settle for it.

A student a few years back had to make that offering of "thanks, but no thanks" to a Saint. She did a spell invoking St. Cajetan to help her get back into the workforce after taking several years off to have a child and raise it until pre-school age. Saint Cajetan is a patron of the unemployed and also founded a bank in 1539 called the Banco della Pieta to help the poor. That bank has evolved over the last 500 years and is still in existence today as the Banco di Napoli. He is excellent at providing boons that not only keep people out of poverty, but generate real wealth.

She did a series of energetic pillar and spheres[1] workings, as well as offerings to amplify her power to "be heard" by the Saint, then asked for a job that paid her a six-figure salary. It was more than she felt she deserved, but she was determined to go big or go home. By the end of the novena, she received the offer she needed from an old employer, as well as leads on childcare options. To turn her back on this must seem like sacrilege to some, but that is exactly what she did.

When the offering was staring her in the face, and the thought of returning to a 50-hour-a-week job was a reality she decided she couldn't do, so she went back to St. Cajetan and asked for the same salary, but to work no more than *32 hours a week total, with the ability to work some of those hours from home.*

Imagine the *balls* this took! Did she think she somehow deserved this? No. She just wanted it and was willing to risk the offer on it. She re-formed her statement of intent to include it, and lo and behold, she got it. If she had just assumed that the good Saint knows what's best, and that you need to take whatever result a spirit or spell grants, she would never have gotten what she really wanted and was capable of.

Sovereignty and Teachers

Of course, it is not just spirits that we need to maintain our sovereignty with; it is human teachers as well. There is not enough room in 12 of these books to list the names of all the spiritual teachers who have abused their positions of authority to get their hands on the wallets or sex organs of their followers. This year has seen scandals in the pagan, Buddhist, and Catholic worlds around such issues. I believe that mentors are a blessing, and a good teacher should be honored, but there is no excuse for abuse.

Sometimes we hand over our own sovereignty over ourselves without thinking much about it. In these cases, it is not just the teacher that is responsible, but us. I remember a conversation with a young Lama that I won't name. He spent his entire life as a monk, but he told me students came to him all the time for advice on marriage and business. He would advise people as best he could according to the teachings of the Dharma, and when appropriate, he would perform Tibetan Mo divination. Ultimately though, these are two areas of life that, as a monk, he really doesn't know anything about, and he is concerned that students perceive his words as having more weight than they really should because of his position. If he is uncomfortable with the amount of blind faith that gets aimed at him, imagine what less scrupulous people get up to.

I do whatever I can to discourage people thinking of me as inscrutable, but this kind of thing even happens to me. Once someone emailed me with a question, and then took the lack of response as some kind of wise message to look within. They wrote later to thank me for my wisdom because ultimately, they solved their own problem. That's great, but I felt I had to correct them; I had simply missed their email. I am not so enigmatic as to work in ways that are *that* mysterious.

Karma Avoidance

Probably the biggest reason that people turn their sovereignty over in Sorcery is the avoidance of responsibility and Karma. Remember those weasely modifiers we talked about back in Key 6? I see people all the time turn over their sovereignty, trying to get around the ethical issues that come with spells by using the modifier: "If it be your will." This usually goes at the end of a prayer or invocation to a God, spirit, Saint, or power that you are calling upon. People have explained to me that if they put this statement in, it absolves them from any kind of ethical responsibility because it is ultimately the will of that deity and not them. Sorry, I'm not buying it. There are a couple things wrong with this.

If you are doing a spell, it is usually more active than just a simple prayer. You *intend* for a certain result to come about, so you don't get to wash your hands just because at the end you said, "Thy will be done." If you go see a hitman (spirit), and tell him about this guy that you would love to see iced (your spell goal), and leave a pile of money (offering), but say, "You do what you think is right," that doesn't absolve you from any moral responsibility—you still just hired a hit man.

Magic is about responsibility. It is about establishing your agency in the world and owning it. You are not just begging for something to happen if God wants it to—you are an active participant in making it happen. That's Sorcery for you.

Now, you might be paranoid at this point and think, "Oh, my God, I have to give up Magic because I might hurt someone with my actions." But you are always running the risk of that, Magic or not. That is how this hard-edged world of ours works. Every action affects other people. It's just that with Magic, we have sort of X factor in our pockets that does not conform neatly to the rules.

You are responsible for what you do. You don't get to absolve yourself from Karma by turning that over. Sovereignty implies owning your actions.

Exercise Your Agency

One of the apparent paradoxes of Magic is that we often call upon Cosmic forces that are so far beyond our ordinary perception that they inspire worship and awe, and ask them to help us with stuff that is, from a cosmic standpoint, relatively petty nonsense. Hekate is a Goddess so mysterious as to almost defy description, yet she has been called upon in defixiones tablets to curse neighbors and fix horse races. Jesus is of course seen by Christians as the incarnation of the God Most High, but Harry M. Hyatt recorded spells from the 1930s that call upon him to hot foot enemies in the direction that you fire your shotgun. Kurukulla is an ancient Goddess who can lead you to full Buddhahood, but you can pay to have a group of monks perform her puja to help you get laid.

What gives? Why would spirits and entities like this allow us to call upon them for petty things, and sometimes even acts that might be considered immoral?

The answer is that we each have our own agency, and the Magic is largely mechanistic. Hekate is indeed cosmic in scope, so much so that she is not particularly interested in how you settle your dispute with your coworker. You make offerings; you do the rituals; she grants the request. That's how it works most of the time.

The Take-Away

This key is about taking responsibility and maintaining your sovereignty. Harold wants to stick pins in someone but wants Salphegor to take responsibility so that his hands are clean. Our demon reminds him that it's his party, his responsibility, and his sovereignty.

Just remember that you hold the agency here. You hold the sovereignty. Don't yield your life over to spirits to make decisions for you. Work with them, even serve them, but maintain your own sovereignty and decisions. That is what Sorcery is here for.

Parting Words

It has been almost exactly 30 years since I tore open the cellophane wrapper on my first Tarot Deck. Thirty years since reading my first books on Magic.[1] Thirty years since I first cast a circle, lit a candle, and asked a spirit to put an extra $50 in my hand—money that came from a found wallet just a few days later.

During the last three decades, I have studied with enterprising Rootworkers, renegade priests, and talky Order initiates who loved trading in secrets. I have gotten drunk with loose-lipped Lamas, done Magic with Catholic priests and Satanists in the same room, and lived for a month with a verifiable wizard. I have been to 21 countries and traveled to caves rumored to be gateways to hell, icebergs whispered to hold entrances to the Devil's school, and mountains where Magicians did battle for the fate of nations. I have been initiated into Magical orders, tantric lineages, pagan lines both ancient and modern, and even consecrated as a Bishop.

I have seen crazy inexplicable paranormal events and things that can only be called miracles. I have also seen enough to know that you cannot count on those to save you in a pinch or to build a life around. If you want Magic to work, you have to work it wisely in conjunction with living the rest of your life wisely as well.

There is no Magic Magic. That's not a typo. It means that there is no one piece of Magic that is more Magical than the rest, no one spell or spirit that is going to accomplish the life changes that the others have not.

I know more Magic than I can ever use in this life, and chances are you do too. If you don't, then stick with it for a few years and you will. But there is no one Magic bit of Magic that will make it all work out. The spells work fine; it's how you use them that makes the difference. The methods are many but the principals are few. These 21 Keys have helped me guide myself and my students to lives that are successful in money, in love, and in spiritual awakening. Now the Keys are yours.

Appendix 1:
The Seal of Manifestation

The sigil that graces the cover of this book was received in working between me and Matthew Brownlee. It is one of a set of seals that affects the movement of Magic itself. To understand this seal, you need to follow its path and understand the layers that Magic moves through.

Begin at the circle on the right. This is what you intend to manifest; it's off to the side because it lies in an alternate probable future from the ones that are currently lined up to become reality. This seal pulls it inward and lifts it up to receive the blessings of spirit. It then drives it down harder into manifestation, "earthing it" to physicality and making it more tangible. It lifts it up again for blessing and elevation, then down once more forming a shape that starts to recall a pentagram—probably the most recognizable symbol for Magic in the Western traditions. Rather than completing a pentagram, however, the seal spirals the Sorcery forth into time. If you concentrate on the spiral, you can start to see a depth to the sigil that moves beyond the two dimensions it appears in. This speaks to the cyclical nature of reality, and our spell is launched into manifestation.

You can utilize this seal however you like—on petitions, on talismans, traced in the air, or held in the mind. It is a catalyst for Sorcery, and aids in the speed of manifestation as well as controlling some of the Rhizomic spread.

Appendix 2: 7 Keys for Successful Divination

Originally I was going to include divination as one of the keys of Spellcrafting, but I decided to leave it out because ultimately spells are about making things happen, whereas divination is about prediction and insight.

Of course, I use divination in my work and thought it might be helpful to share a few keys that have improved my skills and success:

1. **Better to be wrong than vague.** Everyone is afraid of being wrong when they divine, and so often people couch their divination in such vague terms that no matter what happens, they can look back and claim that they were right. Don't do this. Vague information isn't actionable or helpful. It's better to be detailed and be wrong. Lots of professionals can be wrong—just look at the success rate of mutual fund managers and lawyers.

2. **Be brutal.** No one likes delivering unpleasant news, but in the end, its better to deliver unpleasant tidings than it is to pretend like everything is fine. Yes, the death card can mean great change, but if the question was about someone's health, that great change is possibly exactly what it looks like.

3. **Be literal.** Divination is sometimes *very* literal. It is often as literal as it can possibly be. I once drew the Pope card for someone who, unbeknownst to me, was scheduled to have an audience with the Pope in a month. Another time I drew the Lovers card, which shows a man choosing between two women. This querent had literally been in a three way that week.

4. **Remember the question.** I meet readers all the time who forget to interpret the cards or the runes or whatever it is that they read with, in the light of the question that was asked. They read like they are just giving a general reading. The question is what will determine the meaning of the card, far more than the little white book your deck came with. One of the reasons that I favor Marseilles-style decks is that the cards are plainer and it's easier to focus on the person in front of me and their problem, rather than the esoteric onslaught of runes and symbols and letters and sigils that have been packed into Occult decks, or whatever fun theme your deck is based on. Hello Kitty Tarots are fun, but is that helping your divination?

5. **Get readings from others.** As I have said, no one likes delivering unpleasant news. We especially don't like delivering it to ourselves. Get readings from other people, preferably ones who are not invested in you hearing only good things.

6. **Gather intelligence.** A single reading is a piece of data. You take that and compare it to other pieces of data. This could be other readings in different styles, but it could also be rumors, insight, analysis, and any other way that you can think of to get information. Actionable intelligence is constructed from multiple corroborating data points.

7. **Practice.** Keep doing it. Follow up with people afterward. It is the only way to get good.

Notes

KEY 1

1. Aleister Crowley, *Magic in Theory and Practice* (New York: Dover, 1976).

2. Donald Michael Kraig, *Modern Magick: Eleven Lessons in the High Magickal Arts* (St. Paul, Minn.: Llewellyn, 1988).

3. Frater U.D., *Secrets of the German Sex Magicians* (St. Paul, Minn.: Llewellyn, 1995).

4. Sara wrote about this in her blog *http://traifbanquet.blogspot. com/2014/07/sabnok-giver-of-castles.html*. You can find more about Sara and her work at *www.mastroszealot.com*.

KEY 3

1. Yes, that L. Ron Hubbard.

2. Learn more about Marjorie Cameron in the film Wormwood Star from 1955 and the Camercon Parsons Foundation: *www.cameron-parsons.org*.

3. For more on Jack Parsons, see *Sex and Rockets* by John Carter.

KEY 6

1. H.B. Kappes and G. Oettingen, "Positive fantasies about idealized futures sap energy," *Journal of Experimental Social Psychology* Volume 47, Issue 4 (July 2011): 719–729.

KEY 11

1. Aleister Crowley, *The Book of the Goetia of Solomon the King* (Magickal Childe facsimile, 1989).

2. Lon Milo DuQuette, *Low Magick: It's All In Your Head...You Just Have No Idea How Big Your Head Is* (Woodbury, Minn.: Llewellyn Publications, 2010).

3. John 10:34, King James Bible.

4. I cover it in my Strategic Sorcery course.

KEY 12

1. Reference to Justice Clarence Thomas asking Anita Hill, "Who has put pubic hair on my Coke?" A reference, some believe, to the practice of feeding a potential lover your sexual hairs to bind them.

2. First appeared in *https://caduceuswild.wordpress.com/2016/04/07/magical-uses-for-dirt*. Quoted with permission from the author who prefers to remain anonymous.

3. For more on this, see *Grimoires: A History of Magic Books* by Owen Davies.

KEY 13

1. William J. Cromie, "Meditation changes temperatures: Mind controls body in extreme experiments," *Harvard University Gazette* (April 18, 2002).

2. Robert Downey Jr. on *Inside the Actors Studio*, 7/9/2006.

KEY 14

1. Carl Gustav Jung, *Memories, Dreams, Reflections* (New York: Vintage Books, 1989).

2. Gilles Deleuze and Félix Guattari, *A Thousand Plateaus: Capitalism and Schizophrenia* (Minneapolis, Minn.: University of Minnesota Press,1987).

3. *Rhizomes: Cultural Studies in Emerging Knowledge* Bowling Green State University (ISSN 1555-9998).

4. Defense.gov news transcript: "DoD News Briefing–Secretary Rumsfeld and Gen. Myers, United States Department of Defense" *http://archive. defense.gov/Transcripts/Transcript.aspx?TranscriptID=2636.*

KEY 15

1. Gabriel appeared to Daniel to explain his visions, to Zechariah to foretell the birth of John the Baptist, to Mary to foretell the birth of Jesus, to Mohammad to deliver the Quran, and to Joseph Smith to deliver the Book of Mormon. Gabriel gets my vote for busiest angel.

KEY 16

1. Gordon White, "Good Spellcasting Means Knowing When to Collapse," Rune Soup blog, May 24, 2010.

KEY 17

1. Helios caught Aphrodite cheating with Ares and told her husband, Hephasteus. In revenge, Aphrodite caused Helios to fall in love with a Persian princess. When Aphrodite then told the King of his daughter taking a Greek God as a lover, he had her killed. Do not mess with Aphrodite.

KEY 18

1. From the back of an Omnipresencia De Dios candle that I purchased at a supermarket.

2. This is so common it has a name: the sunk cost fallacy.

KEY 20

1. St. Cyprian, the five Dzambhalas, Hekate, Jupiter, Astaroth, and Our Lady of Good Remedy. From the outside these have nothing to do with each other, besides the fact that I encountered them all at various times in my life.

2. Austin Carr, "Blockbuster: We Can Beat Bankruptcy and Netflix," Fast Company, August 18, 2010. *www.fastcompany.com/1683812/blockbuster-we-can-beat-bankruptcy-and-netflix*

KEY 21

1. See my book *The Sorcerer's Secrets*.

PARTING WORDS

1. *The Magus* by Francis Barrett and *Mastering Witchcraft* by Paul Huson. I honestly can't remember which came first, but I checked them out of the library on the same day.

About the Author

Jason Miller's (Inominandum) interest in the Occult was sparked by a series of psychic experiences he had when he was just five years old. He took up the practice of both High Magick and Hoodoo Rootworking while still a teenager, learning how ceremonial and folk Magic can work together and complement each other.

He has been involved with a number of orders and groups through the years, always seeking the quintessence of the arte. He has traveled to New Orleans to study Hoodoo, Europe to study Witchcraft and Ceremonial Magick, and Nepal to study Tantra. Miller is an initiated Tantrika in the Nyingma and Bon lineages of Tibet, an ordained Gnostic Bishop, and a member of the Chthonic Ouranian Temple and the Sangreal Sodality.

He is the author of:

- *Protection and Reversal Magick: A Witch's Defense Manual*
- *The Sorcerer's Secrets: Strategies in Practical Magic*
- *Financial Sorcery: Magical Strategies to Create Real and Lasting Wealth*
- The Strategic Sorcery course
- The Strategic Sorcery blog

Miller lives with his wife at the New Jersey shore, where he practices and teaches Magick professionally. Visit him at *www.strategicsorcery.net*

About the Illustrator

Mathew Brownlee is an Occultist and tattoo artist located in Philadelphia. He is a member of the Chthonic Auranian Temple and is a Tantrika in the Nyingma and Bon lineages of Tibet. He is a graduate of the Philadelphia Art Institute and works at Baker Street Tattoo in Media, Pennsylvania.

Visit him at *www.bakerstreettattoo.com*.